The Empath the Sensitive Person

Mastering Emotional Intelligence and Building Strong Relationships by Navigating and Thriving with Empathic Abilities

Richard Banks

© Copyright 2023 by Richard Banks. All right reserved

The content contained within this book may not be reproduced, duplicated or transmitted without direct written permission from the author or the publisher.

Under no circumstances will any blame or legal responsibility be held against the publisher, or author, for any damages, reparation, or monetary loss due to the information contained within this book. Either directly or indirectly.

Legal Notice:

This book is copyright protected. This book is only for personal use. You cannot amend, distribute, sell, use, quote or paraphrase any part, or the content within this book, without the consent of the author or publisher.

Disclaimer Notice:

Please note the information contained within this document is for educational and entertainment purposes only. All effort has been executed to present accurate, up to date, and reliable, complete information. No warranties of any kind are declared or implied. Readers acknowledge that the author is not engaging in the rendering of legal, financial, medical or professional advice. The content within this book has been derived from various sources. Please consult a licensed professional before attempting any techniques outlined in this book.

By reading this document, the reader agrees that under no circumstances is the author responsible for any losses, direct or indirect, which are incurred as a result of the use of the information contained within this document, including, but not limited to, — errors, omissions, or inaccuracies.

Why You Should Read This Book

Are you tired of feeling overwhelmed, out of control, or like a prisoner of your emotions? Have you ever questioned why you are so sensitive to certain things? Have you ever been in a crowded place and felt extremely overwhelmed or uncomfortable? Are you struggling to navigate the complexities of human interaction in our fast-paced, modern world?

Look no further than "The Empath and the Highly Sensitive Person" - the ultimate guide to understanding and managing your emotional sensitivity. Being an empath or a highly sensitive person in a world filled with chaos can be a hard undertaking, but with the correct knowledge and tools you will be able to turn your sensitivity into your very own super power!

With insights rooted in neuroscience, biology, and psychology, Banks provides a comprehensive understanding of the empathic and sensitivity traits, their genetic and environmental factors, and the unique abilities and talents that empaths possess. But this book goes beyond just understanding - it offers practical techniques for managing and regulating your empathy, strengthening your empathic abilities, and finding self-care strategies that work best for you.

This book is not just for individuals struggling with hyper-empathy; it's for anyone seeking to better understand and connect with others on a deeper level. With valuable insights into the role of empathy and sensitivity in leadership and relationships, you'll learn how to use your gifts to create more compassionate and understanding connections with those around you.

Navigating relationships as an empath or highly sensitive person can be difficult, and Banks doesn't shy away from addressing those challenges head-on. From identifying if you are an empath to protecting yourself in relationships and finding supportive communities, this book provides the guidance and tools you need to thrive as a highly sensitive individual.

This book will teach you:

- How to identify if you are an empath or highly sensitive person
- The unique abilities and talents that empaths possess
- Techniques for managing and regulating empathy
- How to develop and strengthen empathic abilities
- Strategies for coping with high sensitivity
- The role of empathy and sensitivity in leadership and relationships
- How to deal with difficult people and insensitive comments

So why should you read " The Empath and the Highly Sensitive Person"? Because it's not just a book - it's a transformative journey that empowers you to harness your emotional sensitivity and connect with the world in a more profound way. It's a guide that can help you live a happier, more fulfilling life, no matter how sensitive you may be.

Unlock the power to control your emotions and take

charge of your life! Don't let your emotions hold you back any longer - seize the opportunity to transform your emotional sensitivity into a strength.

Order your copy today and start your journey towards a more empathic, understanding, and fulfilling life.

.Thank You!

Thank you for your purchase.

I am dedicated to making the most enriching and informational content. I hope it meets your expectations and you gain a lot from it.

Your comments and feedback are important to me because they help me to provide the best material possible. So, if you have any questions or concerns, please email me at richardbanks.books@gmail.com.

Again, thank you for your purchase.

Foreword 13

Introduction 17

Chapter 1: The Empath and the Highly Sensitive 23

Who Are Empaths and Highly Sensitive People? 25

Prevalence and Common Characteristics of Empaths and Highly Sensitive People 28

The Neuroscience and Biology of Empathy and Sensitivity 34

Empathy 35

Sensitivity 37

Genetical and Environmental Factors that Affect Empathic and Sensitivity Traits 38

Genetic Factors 38

Environmental Factors 39

Types of Empaths 40

Chapter 2: Understanding Empathic Abilities 43

The Science Behind Empaths and Empathy 45

How Do Empaths Process and Absorb Emotions from Others? 49

Unique Abilities and Talents Empaths Possess 51

Empaths with Notable Success and Fulfillment in Various Fields 53

The Role of Empathy and Sensitivity in Leadership and Relationships 57

Chapter 3: Recognizing and Developing Empathic Abilities 61

How to Identify if You Are an Empath 63

Techniques for Managing and Regulating Empathy 67

How to Develop and Strengthen Empathic Abilities 71

The Importance of Self-Care for Empaths 74

Empaths' Role in Creating a More Compassionate and Understanding Society 78

Exploring the Positive Aspect of Being an Empath or Highly Sensitive Person 79

Chapter 4: Navigating Relationships as an Empath 83

In What Ways Do Empaths Encounter Difficulties in Relationships? 85

How Can Empaths Use Their Gifts to Connect with Others? 91

In What Ways Can Empaths Protect Themselves in Relationships? 95

Ways to Find and Connect with Other Empaths 100

Self-Assessment Quiz 103

Chapter 5: Understanding and Navigating Highly Sensitive People 113

How to Identify a Highly Sensitive Person in You or Someone You Know 115

Potential Benefits and Challenges of Being an HSP 119

Strategies for Coping with High Sensitivity 123

Importance of Self-Care for HSPs 124

Navigating Relationships as an HSP 126

Chapter 6: Empaths in Society and Culture 131

The Role of Empaths in Different Cultures and Societies Throughout History 133

The Impact of Empaths on Society and Culture 140

What Potential Challenges Do Empaths Face in Our Fast-Paced World? 144

Chapter 7: Navigating Challenges and Harnessing the Strengths and Gifts of Emotional Sensitivity 149

What Strategies Work Best to Manage the Unique Challenges of Empaths and HSPs? 150

How to Deal with Difficult People and Insensitive Comments 157

Should You Find a Supportive Community? 159

How You Can Embrace and Develop Your Empathic Abilities 160

Ways to Encourage and Empower Empaths and HSPs to Accept and Harness Their Traits 162

Exercises for Empaths and Highly Sensitive People 165

Conclusion 169

Bonus Chapter 177

Books by Richard Banks 195

References 197

FOREWORD

I am honored to introduce Richard Bank's groundbreaking work in the field of emotional responsiveness. As a neuropsychologist, I've had the privilege of working with individuals who possess exceptional empathy and sensitivity. In our fast-paced, modern world, these traits are often misunderstood and undervalued.

Bank's practical guide is a valuable resource for those who struggle with heightened emotional responsiveness. His work is easily digestible and provides empowerment to those who need it most. I commend Bank for his contribution to the field and believe that his insights will be invaluable to readers.

- Shawn Messonnier, Ph.D.

Richard Banks' book is a helpful and enlightening

guide that sheds light on the real challenges faced by empaths and highly sensitive people. Banks illustrates how these individuals can form deep connections with others while avoiding common pitfalls in human interaction.

For those who have felt overwhelmed, out of control, or like a prisoner of their emotions, this book provides practical solutions and guidance. As a clinical psychologist, consultant, and speaker, I highly recommend this book to anyone seeking to better understand themselves and their emotional experiences.

- Dr. Brian L. Schwartz

Richard Banks' guidebook, "Empaths and Highly Sensitive People," is an incredibly practical and informative resource for those seeking to understand hyper-empathic states. Banks' clear and authoritative explanation of the empath phenomenon provides valuable insights into how highly empathic individuals can work on self-care and develop more harmonious relationships.

As an author who has explored the intricacies of human emotion in my work, I highly recommend this guidebook as one of the most useful resources available on this topic. Banks' work is a must-read for anyone seeking to better understand the complexities of emotional sensitivity.

- Mark S. Treadwell

Richard Bank's guide to empaths and highly sensitive people is a wonderful resource that provides valuable insights into the challenges faced by individuals who are highly empathic or sensitive. Although I have never been classified as such, I have personally experienced some of the challenges that Banks outlines in his book.

I highly recommend this guide to anyone who is or knows someone who is an empath or highly sensitive person. Banks' book is an excellent guide that offers practical solutions and techniques to help individuals better understand and manage their emotions.

- Dr. John Miller

Richard Bank's book is a must-read for anyone on the journey of self-awareness and higher consciousness. Bank's straightforward and honest approach makes this often-difficult journey simple and accessible.

As a certified empathic coach, I have seen first-hand the benefits of Bank's work in providing support and comfort to those who are highly sensitive. His book is a valuable resource that will bring awareness to millions of sensitive individuals and empower them to navigate their emotions with greater ease and clarity.

- Shashida Alkhateeb

Introduction

"Empathy is seeing with the eyes of another, listening with the ears of another, and feeling with the heart of another." - Alfred Adler

Being an empath or a highly sensitive person can be both a blessing and a burden. On one hand, empathic abilities allow us to connect deeply with others, uniquely feel emotions and energies, and develop a deeper understanding of the world. On the other hand, they can trigger overwhelming emotions that drain our energy levels and negatively affect our relationships, work, and overall well-being.

Undoubtedly, it can be challenging to find balance and peace when navigating the complexities of emotional intelligence (also known as emotional quotient or EQ) and managing the ups and downs of daily life. Studies have shown that empathic individuals experience more burnout and a higher risk of health problems than their peers. Such adverse outcomes stem from the lack of tools and knowledge to overcome emotional challenges.

"The Empath and the Highly Sensitive Person" is designed to help individuals understand their emphatic abilities, develop emotional intelligence, and create healthy relationships. It provides practical strategies, tips, and exercises to help you harness your strengths, overcome your shortcomings, build resilience, and succeed in all aspects of life.

This book contains a wide range of topics, including self-care, communication skills, boundary-setting, and much more. Each section offers a roadmap to understanding emotional quotient and provides a solid foundation for exponential growth in your personal and professional life.

By reading this guide, you will:

- Develop a deeper understanding of your empathic abilities and how they impact your emotions, thoughts, and relationships.
- Learn how to manage and control your emotions and energy to avoid feeling overwhelmed and drained.
- Enhance your emotional intelligence and develop stronger, more fulfilling relationships.
- Discover the power of empathy and learn how to use it to your advantage.
- Increase your confidence and self-awareness, as well as overcome self-doubt and negative beliefs.
- Better understand and navigate relationships with others who may not understand your empathic abilities.
- Recharge your energy and protect your boundaries to maintain balance and well-being.
- Develop a sense of purpose and fulfillment as you learn to use your abilities for the good of yourself and others.

This book is not just a theory or an abstract concept. It's a practical guide that draws upon the author's expertise and experience, having helped countless individuals find their place in the world. You will find real-life stories, testimonials, and case studies of people who have successfully applied the strategies and exercises described in this book. A number of these individuals have seen improvements in their careers, finances, physical health, relationships, and finding a better sense of balance and harmony.

As you read through the book, you'll be encouraged, motivated, and empowered to make positive changes. You will be more in touch with yourself and better equipped to manage your emotions. While it's true that empathy is a powerful tool for building strong relationships, it can also result in feelings of loneliness, stress, and exhaustion if not properly managed.

You may struggle to maintain long-term, healthy relationships because you are always looking out for others and placing your own needs on the back burner. You may also experience anxiety, anger, sadness, or rage due to strong emotions, or develop low self-esteem and experience low self-confidence. The longer you wait to address these issues, the harder it becomes to live the life you desire and deserve.

Your mental and physical health could be jeopardized if you don't find a way to address your challenges. Conditions like chronic stress and emotional exhaustion can lead to various physical health problems, including headaches, insomnia, heart disease, and depression. The good news is, it's never too late to take control of your life as an emphatic individual. The sooner you start, the sooner you'll be able to harness the power of your abilities and live a fulfilling, meaningful life.

Imagine a future where you wake up each morning feeling energized, ready to start the day, and take on whatever challenges come your way. Imagine how your relationships will be affected when you can connect with people meaningfully and be understood in return. Would that be worth it? What's more, you'll have more energy to care for yourself and spend quality time with your loved ones.

Don't wait any longer to discover the power of emotional intelligence and put yourself on the path to achieving your highest potential. Understand that empathy is something you are born with. Some people naturally have more of it than others, while a minority have none. But every one of us can learn to be kind and compassionate to ourselves and others. It boils down to self-awareness and finding the right strategies and tools to become more aware of your emotions and deal with challenges healthily.

This book does not require you to be an empath to profit from it. While certain strategies are unique to empaths, most of the knowledge applies to anyone seeking a healthy and balanced life. So, what are you waiting for?

Let's get started!

Chapter 1: The Empath and the Highly Sensitive

"Empaths are not victims of their sensitivity, but rather powerful individuals who can harness their gifts to make a difference in the world." - Dr. Elaine Aron

Have you ever noticed how much you pick up on other people's emotions through their actions? It might be the way a stranger in a restaurant looks away as you order your food or the sound of the grocery store attendant grumbling about how slow the line moves. Perhaps, you overhear a co-worker discussing their marriage and can sense their anxiety. Or maybe you notice a change in facial expression across the room and start to feel your heart racing.

Maybe you have a special friend, and you can feel the energy coming off them like a wave. When they talk about their problems, you suddenly feel depressed and drained. It could be the way a loved one looks at you that makes you feel an overwhelming sense of love and gratitude. You notice all these things and wonder why you always seem to be so affected by other people. Why do you feel sad for this person or happy for that one?

Then you realize that you've always had this unique ability to empathize. But, like many of us, you've also been told that you're supposed to "suck it up" and be tougher. To put it bluntly, you've been encouraged to act like everyone else and ignore these feelings of empathy. After all, we live in a "dog-eat-dog society," and tough times never last, but tough people do, right?

You've been told that "sucking it up" isn't just a cliché, but it's the only way to survive in this harsh world. What if I told you that you were living your life based on a false belief? What if there is a way to embrace your ability to empathize and use it to better the world, one person at a time? Well, it's time to break that cycle and learn how to utilize your innate empathic abilities.

However, before you own up to your persona, believing that being an empath and a highly sensitive person is the same thing, I'd like to share an incredibly liberating idea that will revolutionize your perception of these two distinct personality types. Yes, they may sound similar, but they are poles apart.

Who Are Empaths and Highly Sensitive People?

Empaths and highly sensitive people (HSP) are terms used to describe individuals with a strong sense of empathy and awareness. While empathy refers to the ability to understand and share the feelings of others, high sensitivity refers to a tendency to pick up on stimuli in the environment easily.

Scratching beneath the surface, empaths have a "sixth

sense," formally described as a deep level of emotional awareness. This helps them understand human feelings and intentions (both positive and negative). They have the ability to read people's non-verbal cues and body language better than anyone else in the room. In most cases, they process emotions unconsciously, which in the absence of an active protective psychological barrier, can take a heavy toll on their well-being.

For empaths, emotional resonance (the core psychological construct of compassion and altruism) is a fundamental aspect of communication. As such, it is not surprising to find that they can be great listeners and often have a knack for understanding people's needs. They are the typical "I feel your pain" or "You're not alone" types. For the most part, this comes as no surprise, as they often come across as overly friendly and caring to those around them.

A typical example is an empath on a crowded bus. They can tell the person beside them is exhausted and would die for a seat. In such situations, they are not thinking about their discomfort but rather the need to help this other person. Their sympathetic mind kicks in, and they offer the individual their seat. It comes naturally to them; such an interaction doesn't hurt or affect their emotions.

On the other hand, highly sensitive persons are highly attuned to their environment with regard to external stimuli such as visual, auditory, olfactory, and gustatory. They can experience negative or uncomfortable sensations due to loud noise, bright lights, and strong smells. They constantly feel bombarded by the world around them and tend to shut down in such environments.

For example, a highly sensitive person's anxiety can be triggered by seemingly benign situations such as a noisy room or waiting in a long queue. This is because they tend to take in more than the average person and experience overstimulation in their nervous system. Their sensitivity stems from an innate need to protect themselves from such experiences, often resulting in self-imposed emotional isolation.

PREVALENCE AND COMMON CHARACTERISTICS OF EMPATHS AND HIGHLY SENSITIVE PEOPLE

About 20% of the population can be described as highly sensitive persons. And while 70% of these individuals are introverts, the other 30% are extroverts. However, not all introverts are highly sensitive or empathic.

Research indicates that women are more likely to be empaths or HSPs than men, which may be due to the social role of women often being nurturing and self-sacrificing.

The fundamental reasoning for this is blamed on cultural expectations that drive men to act "tough." As a result, they repress their sensitivity, which isn't only unnatural but also unhealthy and unfulfilling.

This is the story of Alexander Hopwood, a dark empath and military consultant who shared his experience with me about how suppressing his empathic side nearly drove him to suicide. A dark empath typically refers to someone who possesses the ability to empathize with others but uses it for manipulative or harmful purposes. This could be someone who understands the emotions and vulnerabilities of others but instead of using that understanding to help them, they use it to control or exploit them.

Alexander Hopwood was not born a dark empath, as his psychologist had diagnosed. As a child, he felt genuine empathy and believed that he could make the world a better place. However, his dad would belittle and hit him at any opportunity for being an overly sensitive "crybaby" and a "wimp". At such an early age, this abuse severely damaged Hopwood's sense of self-worth and caused him to care less.

His action led to further emotional damage, isolation, and depression. As he grew older, he found it challenging to hold relationships. According to him, he lied and manipulated his partner in his previous relationship. Yet, the only thing that bothered him was moving out and not having the same financial support.

Due to his father's abusive behavior, Hopwood was left with a damaged emotional radar. As such, he never felt genuine love for his then-girlfriend. Believing that she was easy to manipulate, he took advantage of her emotions. There were moments when he considered turning a new leaf, but in his words, "Something would come up, and I'd just go back to my old ways."

His moods wavered like a turbulent sea. He could give anyone the moon one minute and then take it away the next, whenever he pleased. Despite being an extrovert, he couldn't keep friends for long since he became easily bored. Deep down, he considered his actions as a way to escape his mind. His intimacy with ladies provided a gateway for him to implant dreadful ideas that he would later implement during their vulnerable moments. It worked as he knew how to read a room, and always had precisely the right words.

Alcohol and drugs couldn't numb the emotional pain of Hopwood's past, and at one point, he contemplated committing suicide. However, all that changed following an accidental encounter with another empath. Hopwood struck up a conversation with the stranger after a couple of drinks. He discovered they were on the same level emotionally, something he hadn't witnessed in a long time.

"I told her all about my past and how bad I was to people. She listened with zero judgment and told me, 'There's nothing wrong with you, Alexander. You were just raised wrong by someone who never understood what true emotions felt like. All you need is to forgive yourself and embrace who you really are.'"

Hopwood awoke the following day with a sense of peace. Even though he never saw the stranger again, that day marked the start of a new chapter in his life. He slowly began to embrace his sensitivity and, with the help of a professional counselor, learned how to channel his innate ability to help others. Today, Hopwood feels deeply connected to his empathic side and works as a professional development coach to help others live happier and more balanced lives.

When it comes to what makes a person an empath or highly sensitive, there are specific characteristics to consider.

Empaths

- Extreme sensitivity to emotions: Empaths have an innate ability to sense other people's emotions, even if such feelings are not explicitly expressed.
- Strong compassion: Empaths often experience a strong urge to help others and alleviate their suffering.
- Easily overwhelmed: Empaths can quickly become overwhelmed in emotionally charged situations due to their heightened sensitivity to emotions.
- Tendency to absorb others' emotions: When empaths take on the emotions of others as their own, they often end up physically and emotionally exhausted.
- Difficulty setting boundaries: It is often difficult for an empath to say 'no' to the requests of their friends, family, and co-workers, even when their time and energy levels are stretched to the max.

Highly Sensitive People

The key aspects of high sensitivity can be summarized in four letters:

D, O, E, and S.

Depth of processing

Overstimulation

Emotional reactivity

Sensing the subtle

A broader explanation of the qualities of an empath is as follows:

- Sensitivity to stimuli: Highly sensitive people process sensory input at a much deeper level. They are aware of their surroundings and often notice unusual details that may be missed by others. As such, they are easily overwhelmed by too much information.

- Deep thinking and reflection: Introspection is a common characteristic of HSPs, which enables them to think deeply and reflect on their feelings, experiences, and surroundings.
- Strong empathy: Like empaths, highly sensitive people have a strong capacity for empathy and can quickly become affected by the emotions of others.
- Need for solitude: High levels of stimulation can be exhausting for highly sensitive people, who often require isolation and quiet time to recharge.

THE NEUROSCIENCE AND BIOLOGY OF EMPATHY AND SENSITIVITY

When we talk about empathy and sensitivity, we're talking about a type of consciousness where we connect with the feelings and thoughts of others and external stimuli from our surroundings. From a scientific standpoint, empathy and sensitivity are influenced by a complex interplay of biological and neurological factors, including genetics, hormones, and brain structure and function.

The underlying mechanisms involved in these processes are complex and still not fully understood. However, researchers have made significant progress in identifying some key regions at play.

EMPATHY

MIRROR NEURON SYSTEM

The mirror neuron system, located in the frontal and parietal cortex, is thought to play a crucial role in empathy. This system is activated when we observe or imagine the actions or emotions of others and allows us to understand and experience their feelings as if they were our own.

LIMBIC SYSTEM

The limbic system, including the amygdala and the anterior cingulate cortex, processes emotions and regulates our emotional responses. Think of it as the body's emotional control center. The amygdala is essential when it comes to empathizing with other people's emotional states, as well as helping us to detect dangerous or potentially harmful situations.

The anterior cingulate cortex is involved in self-awareness and higher-level functions such as planning, organization, and problem-solving. It is activated when we make decisions. The limbic system may be more active in empaths, allowing them to better experience and understand other people's situations.

Prefrontal Cortex

The prefrontal cortex, located at the front of the brain, shares similar roles with the anterior cingulate cortex. It is responsible for executive functions, including decision-making and social cognition. Researchers suggest that this region may also play a role in empathy by integrating information regarding the emotions and intentions of others.

Sensitivity

Nervous System

The nervous system plays a critical role in sensitivity. Highly sensitive individuals may have a nervous system that is more easily aroused and takes longer to return to a baseline state after being exposed to stimuli.

Genetics

Some evidence suggests that sensitivity may have a genetic basis. Several genes, especially those involved in regulating our stress response, may play a role in determining individual variations in sensitivity — more on this in the next section.

Hormonal Factors

Certain hormones are believed to have an impact on sensitivity. Low levels of serotonin, the neurotransmitter that controls mood, may increase sensitivity to stimuli. Likewise, high levels of cortisol, a stress hormone, can produce the same effect.

Genetical and Environmental Factors that Affect Empathic and Sensitivity Traits

The development of our empathic and sensitivity traits and their expression under various conditions depends largely on our genetic makeup, the environment we live in, and the psychological process we develop throughout our lives.

Genetic Factors

Heritability

Empathy and sensitivity have been shown to have moderate to high heritability, meaning that these traits are partially influenced by genetics.

Candidate Genes

Several candidate genes have been identified that may play a role in the development of empathic and sensitivity traits, including genes involved in regulating stress response, brain development, and neurotransmitter function.

Environmental Factors

Childhood Experiences

Our experiences in the formative years, such as abuse, neglect, or trauma, can influence how we develop empathy and sensitivity, as was the case with Alexander Hopwood. Those who grow up in environments characterized by emotional neglect or abuse may develop a heightened sensitivity to emotions as a survival mechanism.

Parenting Style

How a child is raised can also influence how sensitive or empathetic the individual becomes. Strong empathic qualities are more likely to emerge in children who are nurtured in caring and supporting environments.

Socialization

Children exposed to various experiences and cultures who are taught to value empathy and compassion are more likely to become empaths and highly sensitive people.

Life Experiences

Those who live through hardships and trauma can develop additional layers of empathy and sensitivity, which are especially helpful when dealing with others. For example, an employee who was once fired may develop a strong sense of empathy towards those mistreated by their employers, as they can better relate to their situation.

Types of Empaths

Although there isn't a definitive list of empath types, some people categorize these individuals into groups based on how they experience empathy. A few examples of widely known types are:

Emotional Empath

An emotional empath is highly sensitive to the emotions of others and can easily absorb, internalize, or project these emotions onto themselves. If not managed properly, this can leave them feeling drained and empty.

Physical Empath

A physical empath feels the physical sensations and pains of others. For example, they may find themselves experiencing cramps, headaches, muscle spasms, or exhaustion after being around someone who has a cold or is sick. A physical empath's body is often a mess due to having to be on high alert for the physical and emotional needs of others.

Cognitive Empath

People with this trait can understand the perspectives and thought processes of others. For example, if a friend's school admission application was denied, a cognitive empath would easily see that the individual is hurting and understand why.

Nature Empath

Nature empaths are strongly drawn to the beauty of nature, including plants and animals, and find a great amount of peace in the natural world. In many cases, they are the ones to organize hikes or other outdoor activities because they feel so connected to the earth.

Intuitive Empath

Empaths in this group are known to have a "sixth" sense. Due to their reliance on their inner voice, they may notice things going on with people that no one else seems to see. They are often intuitive and deeply connected to the spiritual realms. This trait helps them develop their empathic gifts, even before they become aware of it.

An empath may not always have a ready explanation for their feelings. Perhaps, they feel a heaviness or great depth of sadness, only to find out later about the grief and loss recently experienced by a friend or colleague.

Chapter 2: Understanding Empathic Abilities

"Empaths have the ability to read between the lines, but we must also learn to listen to what our own bodies are telling us." - Aletheia Luna

Tapping into your empathic abilities can help you become a better listener, more attuned to the needs of others, and more in tune with your surroundings. On a fundamental level, you might be able to tell that someone is being affected by something, but this does not mean you can automatically determine what is to blame.

The degree to which you feel the emotions of others and whether you use this ability to help others depends on a variety of factors. While you may have difficulty explaining your empathic abilities, it is important to understand that everyone has a unique sensitivity inherent in our biology. This is part of our survival mechanism. Empaths also have a natural ability to learn and use other people's feelings and thoughts as a way to gain information about the world around them.

This, combined with your ability to be in the moment, enables you to develop a powerful toolset that will help you work with other people and support them in times of need. Simply put, when you understand what others feel and why, you can be that knight in shining armor. That's why sometimes you hear words like, "He really gets me." Without this trait, you would most likely become that "insensitive" person no one wants to be around.

The Science Behind Empaths and Empathy

Some current scientific studies support the existence of empathic abilities, and several recent discoveries in neuroscience and psychology are shedding light on this fascinating subject. One of the early studies of empathy focused primarily on honesty and involved a series of two-year-long experiments in which a group of researchers tried to assess how willing people were to return a lost wallet found on the street.

According to the researchers, a person's response to finding the wallet would depend on whether it was empty. The researchers assumed that putting money in a wallet would make people less likely to return it because the payoff would be more significant. With 17,000 "lost" wallets dropped off in 40 countries during the study period, the researchers discovered that people were likelier to report a lost wallet with more money than a wallet with little to no cash.

Based on the collated data, 46% of empty wallets, 61%

of those with $13, and 72% with nearly $100 were reported. Three factors suggested the reason behind such honesty: altruism, wealth, and education, with altruism being most highly correlated with honesty.

As highlighted in the first chapter, altruism has its psychological construct embedded in emotional resonance, which is an empath's ability to recognize and experience the physical and emotional states of others. This implies that the individual who reports the missing wallet feels a strong sense of belonging and empathy for the financial plight of the person who lost the wallet, resulting in more honesty, especially when a significant amount of money is involved.

Neural Correlates of Empathy

Studies using functional magnetic resonance imaging (fMRI) have revealed that empathy is associated with increased activity in specific brain regions, including the insula, the anterior cingulate cortex, and the temporoparietal junction. These regions are known to be involved in the processing of emotions, the experience of pain, and the integration of social information.

Genetics

Twin studies have shown that empathy has a moderate to high heritability, suggesting a genetic component to the trait. Additionally, the development of this trait relies on the active presence of candidate genes. These genes include:

- The ASPM gene makes a protein needed for producing new neurons in a developing brain.
- COMT (catechol-O-methyltransferase gene) is involved in the degradation of the neurotransmitters dopamine and norepinephrine. Variations in this gene have been associated with differences in emotional regulation and cognition and may play a role in developing empathy and other social behaviors. This gene is also responsible for stress response.
- Brain-derived neurotrophic factor (BDNF) binds to the brain's receptors and enhances the signals between neurons by promoting growth and preventing premature cell death. This

protein has an impact on how well you can handle stress.

Environmental Factors

Early experiences, parental methods, socialization, and life events can all influence the development of empathy. An adult who has learned to ignore their feelings may not be able to feel empathy in the same way that an individual with a secure upbringing has. For some people, exposure to adversity can increase sensitivity to the experiences of others.

Social and Cognitive Processes

The complex interplay of social and cognitive processes that go into empathy includes the ability to recognize and comprehend the feelings of others, experience those emotions first-hand, and react in a constructive and supportive manner.

How Do Empaths Process and Absorb Emotions from Others?

As more scientific research has gone into understanding the mechanism behind empathy, studies have found that the process involves the activation of brain regions involved in emotional processing. The anterior cingulate cortex and the insula are regions that react to stimuli, including vocal cues, facial expressions, and body language. They aid in your ability to empathize with others.

Empathy also involves the mirror neuron system, a network of neurons that comes to life when we perform a particular action or observe others performing it. With this system, we can simulate other people's behaviors, using our bodies and minds as proxies. This makes us understand and respond to their emotions better. The degree to which an empath may display this attribute is determined by a variety of conditions, including stress, anxiety, and emotional management.

It is possible to pick up on other people's emotions

intuitively and sensorily. For example, you may experience a visceral reaction to someone else's feelings, such as feeling uneasy when that person feels anxious. To paint a clearer picture, imagine being invited alongside a stranger to a place you are not familiar with. On the way there, you can easily sense that the other person is nervous.

The individual may be having second thoughts about the invitation because you can sense their discomfort. As a result, you might also begin to feel uncomfortable, a presentiment that wasn't there before. It is an automatic, emotional reaction to a person's feeling, which you identify as a sense of uneasiness. You might not be able to say what triggered the change, but you know it has something to do with the person who invited you.

Additionally, empaths may also use their intuition to pick up on the emotional state of others, even if they are not physically present. That means you can read the mind of the person who has lost a wallet and feel what he may feel if the situation were reversed.

However, this heightened sensitivity to the emotions of others can also be challenging for empaths. They can easily become overwhelmed by the emotions of others and may struggle to distinguish their own feelings from those of others. This can lead to feeling burnt out and exhausted.

UNIQUE ABILITIES AND TALENTS EMPATHS POSSESS

Empaths are the superheroes of our world. They have the superpower to "see" the world through the eyes of others, "hear" what others may not be able to express, sense their pain and suffering, and take action. Their ability to "feel with their whole being" makes them better spouses, partners, friends, and co-workers. Some extra-ordinary qualities these people possess include:

EMOTIONAL INTELLIGENCE

Empaths are sensitive to other people's emotions and can quickly detect and respond to them. This helps them to establish strong and meaningful relationships.

Empathy

As the name suggests, empaths have a strong capacity for empathy. They have no problem putting themselves in the shoes of other people. An empath will tell you, "I have been there," and will devise ways to improve your situation. This trait makes them valuable.

Intuition

Have you ever had that grandparent or parent who knew what was wrong with you even before you said it? To them, you were a transparent sheet of glass — no hiding whatsoever. For these individuals, intuition has been their superpower for a long time. They have that inner sense or "gut instinct" about something or someone and may even predict future outcomes. The ability to intuit people's motivations and desires comes naturally to them.

Healing

Empaths are naturally compassionate and considerate, making them more inclined to provide comfort, peace, and love to others as support. They are friends who will stick around when you are in emotional pain.

Creativity

Empaths often turn to their creative side as a form of expression. They are not afraid to explore their feelings, allowing them to create deeply meaningful and impactful works of art, poems, songs, stories, and other forms of expression.

Empaths with Notable Success and Fulfillment in Various Fields

Empaths can and do play different roles in our society. Some have used their intuition, empathy, and creative talent to make a significant difference in their communities and the lives of those around them, while others have made an impressive mark in the professional arena. Let's take a look at some of these success stories.

Carl Jung (Psychology)

Carl Jung was a Swiss psychiatrist and psychoanalyst who helped to establish modern psychology. He was known for his empathetic approach to therapy and his ability to connect deeply with his patients, which enabled him to provide them with effective and meaningful treatment. Jung believed that the key to understanding human behavior was to look at the unconscious mind, a technique he used on his patients to help them deal with unresolved issues and psychological problems. Very few people know that he was also an artist, craftsman, builder, and writer.

Vincent Van Gogh (Art)

Vincent Van Gogh was a post-impressionist painter recognized for his emotionally charged and passionate paintings. He was often referred to as an "emotional visionary," considering he could express the emotions of those around him in his artworks.

One of his pieces, Old Man in Sorrow (On the Threshold of Eternity), depicts the mental suffering and despair he experienced in his final months in Auvers-sur-Oise. His affinity for the use of vibrant and dramatic colors was a reflection of his strong emotions.

John Lennon (Music)

John Lennon was a member of the Beatles, one of the most successful and influential musical groups of all time. He was known for his empathetic and socially conscious lyrics, which spoke to the emotions and experiences of people worldwide.

Lennon used his music to address important social issues and inspire change. His empathic trait helped him connect with his audience on a deep and meaningful level.

Oprah Winfrey (Business)

Oprah Winfrey is an author, actor, producer, talk show host, and philanthropist who has made significant contributions to television and business. Her ability to recognize people's weaknesses and needs was a skill that served her well in her career.

In addition to providing individuals with an opportunity to become a success story, Oprah's compassionate nature also inspires many to pursue their own business aspirations. She is also well known for her charitable work, supporting countless causes and organizations.

Nelson Mandela (Politics)

Nelson Mandela was the first black president of South Africa. He is celebrated for forgiving his former adversaries after serving 27 years in prison for his efforts to end apartheid. His sensitivity was shown in his courage and compassion for the people of South Africa.

During his acceptance speech after being elected president in 1994, he emphasized that his country's triumph had come at a high price and that he would lead the country from a place of reconciliation.

The Role of Empathy and Sensitivity in Leadership and Relationships

Empathy is identifying, appreciating, and responding to another person's feelings. It is a type of unconditional love that allows you to interact with others more intimately.

In leadership, empathy helps to establish trust, teamwork, and stronger relationships. As a leader, you can understand the viewpoints and needs of your team members and empower them to be an active part of decision-making. In addition, you can create policies that emphasize the well-being of your team.

An empathetic leader encourages a friendly and inclusive work environment by showing interest in the team's experiences, ideas, and concerns. This creates a sense of solidarity within the team and increases productivity.

Empathy is also essential for effective communication.

Expressing your thoughts and ideas is easier when you understand the next person's feelings. This is why many employers and founders emphasize emotional intelligence when selecting candidates for management positions. In their view, building healthy relationships with colleagues, clients, and partners is critical to successful business management.

From a relationship standpoint, empathy helps you to comprehend and share the emotions of your spouse, friend, colleague, or family member. As a couple, you can validate each other's experiences, perspectives, and emotions to feel heard, seen, and cared for.

In addition, empathy can help resolve conflicts and challenges. Rather than judging your spouse's behavior or the other party's actions, you can acknowledge and understand the underlying emotional factors behind the issue and respond constructively.

Sensitivity, on the other hand, determines how leaders connect with others, make decisions, and evaluate the performance of their organizations. For instance, if you have an affinity toward detail, you may be inclined to find flaws in everything. This is a problem for those who like to have a more big-picture, global perspective.

Conversely, if you are principled, you might be inclined to be more rigid and inflexible, leading to conflict and disharmony. In truth, many executives with sensitivity to detail are exceptional decision-makers who can see the big picture instead of getting caught up in the details. They are highly effective at anticipating others' feelings.

These individuals can make people feel at ease and trust their advice. They are also usually adept at developing strategies that appeal to both their internal and external audiences.

Sensitivity is equally important in relationships. It is a predictor of attraction, compatibility, and long-term satisfaction. People who are sensitive to how their actions are perceived tend to be more welcoming, understanding, tolerant, and empathetic. They are also more likely to take a principled stand on issues they care about, such as accountability and respect. As such, they tend to enjoy healthier relationships.

A highly sensitive individual might be more careful on dates when the other person pays the bill and wouldn't want to overspend on the person's budget. In most cases, they would rather offer to pay their share. This also applies to selecting friends. While the highly sensitive person might think of themselves as being more open to others, they will ultimately pick friends who share similar values and beliefs.

The result is a greater sense of meaning and purpose in their relationships, which, in turn, improves their sense of self-worth and well-being.

Chapter 3: Recognizing and Developing Empathic Abilities

"Empaths are the emotional sponges of the world, but we also have the power to transmute negative energy into positive." - Jennifer Soldner

While it is true that we're born with the capacity for empathy, it's also a learned behavior that can be developed over time. Oliver Parer, a building construction manager and engineer, has been successful in doing so through personal experience. Here is his story.

Oliver had extensive experience in residential construction management, which involved meeting with subcontractors, architects, engineers, and real estate developers. However, on each project, there were instances where he found himself facing a series of obstacles, including miscommunication, conflict, and low morale among his team.

Oliver felt as though he were on an island. He couldn't see the big picture of any project and felt left out when it came to critical decisions. He was frustrated because, despite being a leader, he could not effectively lead and guide the team. He had a wealth of construction experience but lacked the business acumen and communication skills to take his company to the next level.

However, a watershed moment in Oliver's life occurred while working on a particularly challenging construction project. He realized that his lack of empathy significantly contributed to his problems. Determined to turn things around, Oliver made a conscious effort to improve his empathic abilities.

He began to pay more attention to nonverbal clues, such as body language. He also actively listened to his colleagues, workers, contractors, and clients, making a point to respond with empathy and understanding. This approach not only improved the dynamics of the construction project, but it also had a profound impact on Oliver's personal life, as he was better able to connect with his family and friends.

Oliver Parer's turning point serves as a reminder of the power of empathy and its ability to transform relationships and create a more peaceful environment. Like him, you can make a conscious effort to develop your empathic skills and enjoy a more prosperous, more rewarding life.

How to Identify if You Are an Empath

Do You Have a Hard Time Not Caring?

You are naturally empathic and sensitive to other people's feelings and emotions, often at the price of your own. You feel pain and discomfort when others are in pain. You are more likely to notice the pain and struggles of others and to try to help them. But your efforts to help others may put you under stress and strain. Even if you desire to reach out, it may be impossible under certain conditions, leaving you feeling frustrated.

Do You Have a Strong Gut Feeling?

Your intuition might be your empath trait at work. Empaths can pick up on subtle cues that give insight into the thoughts of others. Your intuition often tells you whether someone is being truthful or not. You might trust your instincts when making decisions, even if others consider you impulsive.

Do You Struggle with Closeness and Intimacy?

You might be an empath. Maintaining close contact can be challenging and overwhelming for an empath, which can make it difficult to establish romantic relationships. In truth, you strongly desire to connect and build lasting partnerships, but spending too much time with someone can overwhelm you, causing stress and worries about losing yourself in the relationship.

Moreover, you might experience sensory overload or a "frayed nerves" feeling from too much talking or touching. When you try to express your need for alone time, you tend to absorb your partner's hurt feelings, making you even more distressed.

Do You Have a Hard Time in Crowded Places?

You can't stand crowds for an extended period. You feel uneasy in a noisy place because you easily absorb others' emotions and energies, and excessive exposure to negative vibes may leave you drained or ill. Even the sight of a lot of people walking by can make you uncomfortable. You might go to great lengths to avoid busy streets, parties, shopping malls, and events.

Do People Tend to Tell You Their Problems?

Do people seem to seek you out when they have a

problem, even if they have no intention of burdening you? Perhaps they do so because you are an excellent listener who understands their pains and can provide answers. However, constantly listening to people's issues can be exhausting, especially when they divulge personal and sensitive facts about their life. This might leave you feeling overwhelmed and helpless. If unchecked, you may unknowingly expose yourself to manipulation and toxicity.

Do You Find Comfort in Nature?

Nature may be very relaxing for you since it provides a sense of grounding and balance. You might feel comforted by the sound of flowing water, the wind rustling the trees, or the smell of fresh rain. You may appreciate sitting by the ocean, listening to the waves lapping against the shore, or sitting in the woods.

You may want to help those in need, especially animals and the planet. When you notice the anguish of wildlife or nature, you feel an overwhelming sense of sadness and compassion.

Are You Highly Sensitive to Sounds, Smells, or Sensations?

Empaths often have a heightened sensitivity to different stimuli, including sounds, smells, and physical sensations. This can lead to sensory overload and discomfort in crowded or noisy environments. Intense emotions, bright lights, and strong odors could also affect you more easily. As a result, you may need more time to recharge and maintain balance.

Techniques for Managing and Regulating Empathy

Being empathic is a gift, but it can also be a hindrance. If you are an empath, you know how much energy it takes to help others while still managing your emotions. Fortunately, there are some techniques that can help you manage and regulate your empathic tendencies.

SITUATION SELECTION

Situation selection refers to the process of choosing to engage or disengage from situations that may trigger or challenge our empathy. This is an essential aspect of managing and regulating empathy, as it allows us to avoid becoming overwhelmed by situations that may be too emotionally taxing or difficult to handle.

For example, suppose you're feeling particularly sensitive to the emotions of others. In that case, you might choose to avoid watching sad movies or news programs that could trigger feelings of sadness or distress. Or, if you're feeling particularly empathetic towards someone, you might choose to avoid situations that could cause them additional stress or discomfort, such as a difficult conversation or confrontation.

RESPONSE MODULATION

Response modulation is the ability to control and adjust your emotional responses in a given situation. It is an essential aspect of empathy, as it allows you to respond to the emotional needs of others in a more appropriate and helpful manner.

When it comes to empathy, response modulation can help you avoid sucking in all that emotional tension from others and instead respond in a way that is more supportive and understanding. This may include adjusting your tone of voice, body language, and the words you choose to better match the other person's emotional state.

For example, if someone is feeling sad, you might use a soft and comforting tone of voice and offer words of support. If someone is feeling angry, you might use a calm and neutral tone of voice and avoid saying things that could escalate the situation.

SITUATION MODIFICATION

As the name implies, situation modification allows you to change or modify a situation to make it more manageable or appropriate for your empathy. You could decide to change how you interact with others, select a different environment or adjust your expectations and goals in a given situation.

If you are in a meeting and someone is struggling to express themselves, you can suggest taking a break or changing the location to make the situation more relaxed and comfortable for them. Likewise, if you feel overwhelmed by someone's emotions, you could take a step back and recharge or practice mindfulness.

ATTENTIONAL DEPLOYMENT

This technique requires you to direct and focus your attention on certain aspects of an event or interaction. That way, you can attend to the next person's emotional needs without being overwhelmed. For example, if you are conversing with someone who is upset, you might focus your attention on their body language, tone of voice, and words to understand their emotional state better.

You might also focus your attention on regulating your own emotions to respond more appropriately and helpfully. In addition, attentional deployment may involve avoiding distractions and focusing on the present moment to be fully present and engaged with the other person. Certain meditation techniques can help improve your focus.

Cognitive Reappraisal

Cognitive reappraisal is a mental strategy that involves changing the way we interpret and think about a situation. It can help us manage our empathy by allowing us to regulate our emotional reactions to others' experiences.

For example, suppose we witness someone else's suffering, and our automatic response is to feel overwhelmed with sadness and compassion. In that case, cognitive reappraisal might help us to reframe that situation in a way that enables us to approach it more objectively, reducing the intensity of our emotional response.

As a result, we can avoid getting overwhelmed and maintain a more balanced perspective, which can help us be more effective in offering support and empathy.

How to Develop and Strengthen Empathic Abilities

Now that you understand what it means to be an

empath and the techniques for managing and regulating your empathic tendencies, you might want to develop your abilities further. Here are ways to do so:

Cultivate Curiosity

Encouraging an inquisitive mindset helps to increase empathy as it prompts you to seek out and understand different perspectives and experiences. To cultivate curiosity, try asking open-ended questions, actively listening to other people, and practicing active, non-judgmental observation.

Receive Feedback

Feedback helps you understand how others see you and your actions and provides valuable insight into how you can improve your empathic abilities. To begin with, try to create an environment where you are open to receiving feedback and acting on it. By doing so, you can continuously develop and strengthen your empathy.

Step Out of Your Comfort Zone

As the popular saying goes, "A comfort zone is a beautiful place, but nothing grows there." To be truly empathic, you must expose yourself to new people and experiences. Consider volunteering for a cause, trying new activities, and putting yourself in situations where you can interact with people from different backgrounds and perspectives.

Read Widely

Reading about diverse ideas and experiences can broaden your understanding of the world and help you develop empathy. You may get insight into how other people think, feel, and experience life. It begins with picking a book, news article, biography, or even fiction that cuts across various themes and characters.

Examine Your Biases

Many people are treated poorly, overlooked, discriminated against, exploited, harmed, and mistreated for the mistakes of their forebears, the color of their skin, where they come from, the religion they practice, or any other reason. As an empathic person, you have the capacity to identify and acknowledge biases and try to understand their implications. This enables you to empathize with those who are victims of your own biases.

THE IMPORTANCE OF SELF-CARE FOR EMPATHS

Why do empaths need more self-care? This is because you have so much emotional energy to deal with. It's easy to get overwhelmed when you have a lot of empathy, but that is not an excuse for not practicing self-care. Self-care is critical for all people, especially empaths.

When you are stressed, tired, or emotionally depleted, you cannot handle life's challenges and responsibilities. Taking time to nurture and care for yourself is an important self-care activity that all empaths should prioritize. You must care for your mind and body to maintain your empathic abilities. Here are some ways to do so:

Get More Sleep

Research shows that you need more sleep than the average person. Getting between 7 to 9 hours of quality sleep daily will help you feel well-rested and more energetic. Also, when you get enough rest, you will be able to think more clearly, and better problem solve.

Eat Right

Eating the proper diet ensures that you maintain your overall health. You should make sure to eat whole foods such as fresh fruits and vegetables, nuts, seeds, and fish. You should avoid processed foods that contain refined sugars, artificial ingredients, and excessive salts. You should also aim to drink plenty of water, especially when feeling stressed or overwhelmed.

Exercise Regularly

Engaging in regular physical exercise will boost your energy, help you sleep better, and improve your mood. It also helps to regulate your breathing and reduce stress. Aim to do aerobic exercises like walking, running, and swimming at least three times per week.

Reduce Your Intake of Stimulants and Relaxants

Empaths should limit their intake of caffeine, alcohol, nicotine, and other drugs. These substances interfere with the function of the nervous system and can cause mood swings and other changes in your body.

Be Mindful

Being mindful is a type of meditation that involves being in the present moment and using all your senses to observe and appreciate what is happening around you. Mindfulness can regulate your emotions and help you live in the moment. Mindfulness can be used as a tool to help you better manage and regulate your empathic energy.

Practice Relaxation

Learning the art of relaxation and practicing it regularly will help you deal with the stress of life and deal with difficult situations healthily and effectively.

It can help you release tension and reduce your heart rate and blood pressure. You can practice relaxation by slowing down and doing things that bring you joy, such as listening to music, doing some light yoga, or breathing deeply.

Develop a Healthy Relationship with Your Emotions

Empaths feel all emotions very deeply. This can be very overwhelming, particularly when surrounded by people constantly complaining or showing off. As an empath, you need to learn to protect yourself from negative emotions and develop a healthy relationship with your own emotions.

Practice Self-Compassion

You are not alone when trying to navigate the complex world of emotions. Everyone, even the most skilled and experienced, has feelings of fear, inadequacy, insecurity, and self-doubt. But instead of trying to deal with your emotions on your own, why not have compassion and understanding for yourself?

Empaths' Role in Creating a More Compassionate and Understanding Society

Being an empath is a special gift that makes you an important member of society. This is why you have a role to play in making this world a more compassionate and understanding place. A society with these traits will experience reduced conflict, violence, and war.

With more empaths in the world, many of the issues and problems we face as a species will become easier to deal with. For instance, empathy helps you understand other people and make wiser and more informed choices. It is a powerful tool that allows you to become more thoughtful and compassionate.

It also reduces the fear and anxiety that plague people and lead to social dysfunctionalities such as bullying, prejudice, racism, and xenophobia. There will be more understanding and compassion towards the less fortunate members of our society. In the same vein, people won't feel threatened by others who are different from them but will accept differences and see them as a source of richness and beauty.

EXPLORING THE POSITIVE ASPECT OF BEING AN EMPATH OR HIGHLY SENSITIVE PERSON

Being an empath or highly sensitive person may bring with it both challenges and unique strengths. Empathy is a common trait among empaths and highly sensitive individuals, and it allows them to understand and share the feelings of others in a deep and meaningful way. This quality can lead to strong, supportive relationships, as empaths can truly connect with others on an emotional level.

In addition to empathy, highly sensitive individuals often possess strong intuition and can pick up on subtle cues and emotions in others. This heightened sensitivity can give them a deeper understanding of the world and help them make intuitive decisions. Moreover, empaths and highly sensitive people tend to have rich inner lives and are often highly creative. This combination of empathy and creativity can lead to a deeper appreciation for beauty in all forms, including art, nature, and music.

Another positive aspect of being an empath or a highly sensitive person is their capacity for deep thinking and introspection. They are often introspective and have a strong desire to understand themselves and others. This introspective nature can lead to greater self-awareness, personal growth, and a deeper understanding of the human condition.

In addition to these strengths, empaths and highly sensitive individuals tend to have strong values and a deep sense of right and wrong, which can lead to a strong moral compass. They are often guided by their principles and are not afraid to stand up for what they believe in, even in difficult or challenging situations.

Overall, the traits associated with empaths and highly sensitive people bring richness and depth to their lives, leading to greater self-awareness, compassion, and creativity. By understanding their strengths and having proper self-care and support, empaths and highly sensitive individuals can make the most of their amazing qualities and lead fulfilling lives.

Chapter 4: Navigating Relationships as an Empath

"Empaths are the caretakers of the world, but it's important to remember to take care of ourselves too." - Kasey Claytor

There is a notion that empaths can't have a normal relationship; they have to spend all their time shielding the people they care about from the harsh realities of the world. It's a common myth that's spread throughout cultures and millennia, one that I've held myself to for much of my life. It's even reflected in movies and TV shows. Choose a popular Disney,

Marvel, or Hollywood film, and you'll find traces of this thought pattern, where the main character gets sucked into everyone else's drama, often establishing themselves as that knight in shining armor.

You'll also note a lot of tension and emotional suffering in the relationships on screen. This belief is rooted in our need to identify with and feel like we have control over the people we love. It's this type of control that breeds manipulation, jealousy, and other unhealthy relationship patterns. The affected spouse lacks voice and autonomy often becoming resentful and emotionally isolated, making them more miserable over time. This then deteriorates into a toxic and failed relationship that damages everyone.

And the empath? They feel as though they've failed since their entire purpose is to serve others. Their sentiments are exacerbated by the fact that they take on that hurt as their own weight. It's a downward spiral from there. In truth, we can't go around fixing people into what we want them to be. Doing so will only be a train wreck in the making, not just for them but for us as well. Empaths frequently experience high levels of psychic sensitivity. Like a radio, we may pick up on other people's moods, attitudes, and energy.

With that much time spent absorbing other people's emotions and actions, we become more susceptible to absorbing their pain. It's easy to feel overcharged by other people's energies. And sometimes, the empath is the one at the center of that, which snowballs into a mental breakdown. But does this mean that empaths are better off alone? Of course not. Like any quality or characteristic, empathy comes with its own unique set of challenges. However, it's what you do with these challenges that makes the difference. It takes work, no doubt, but the rewards are abundant if you can stay committed.

In What Ways Do Empaths Encounter Difficulties in Relationships?

Empaths encounter various types of relationships in their lives, and while some navigate them easily, others face recurrent difficulties. What are the factors that hinder empaths from successfully managing their relationships?

Unbalanced Prioritization of Spouse's Needs

The idea that empathy is solely about selflessness is an "old wives' tale." That itself is not a problem. Most proponents of this thought, however, overlook the fact that a healthy relationship is one in which everyone feels at ease and on an equal footing. If an empath is so burdened by the next person's needs that they neglect their own, they will end up not only hurting themselves but the people they care about as well.

Many of my clients have confessed that it took them quite a while to realize how deeply they invested in their spouses — emotionally and physically — that they had forgotten about themselves. It's easy to get caught up in meeting other people's needs, especially when you feel like your actions will make a positive impact. For empaths, this kind of compassion is often a driving force behind their desire to help people.

They consider themselves to be caretakers. However, neglecting their needs in the process could lead to mental distress in the long run. It's a fine line to walk between selflessness and putting oneself last. It's an even finer one to walk when the recipient is a loved one.

THE FEAR OF INTIMACY

Since empaths are hyper-sensitive, they tend to feel other people's emotions in a profound way. Intimacy can be a nerve-wracking experience for them as they fear that their feelings will be overwhelmed by the other person. They may also worry that their emotions will not be reciprocated and that they will end up being used. For this reason, they become so protective of their hearts that they fail to open up, which causes great stress.

It is important to note that there is nothing wrong with having these feelings. The issue is when they control and dictate your choices on how you accept people into your life. Maybe you've set up a firewall to protect yourself from hurt, yet it's also blocking your opportunity to grow and learn in the company of others.

You don't need to build this wall or keep it up forever, especially if your significant other or anyone else is patient enough to get you to feel comfortable enough to trust them.

Information Overload

Empaths use a feeling-based or clairsentient (intuition-based) approach to life. Their senses are a valuable resource that could be harnessed and channeled to their advantage. But most of the time, these senses are triggered without being needed. It's like having a phone constantly alerting you to every text, call, and notification you receive. Just as this constant stream of alerts can be overwhelming, so can the continuous stream of emotions and energy that empaths pick up on.

This kind of overload negatively affects the empathic person's life and career. Over time, they may develop a condition known as "introversion," which is when an empath develops a fear of intimacy. It manifests as an extreme dislike for meeting people or even small talk.

If put on the spot, they'll get too nervous to respond.

A good coping mechanism is to learn how to manage your sensitivity consciously. With practice, you can "turn on" your empathic skills when needed and "turn off" when you're already feeling drained.

ABSENCE OF EMOTIONAL BOUNDARIES

The desire to help others is intense in empaths, so it doesn't come as a surprise that they may struggle to draw the line between being there for others and taking on too much. They may be so willing to fulfill the next person's needs that they are taken advantage of. This is especially true when they don't have clear emotional boundaries in place.

This was the case of a client of mine, Sarah, who had a friend, Rachel, who was going through a rough patch in her life. Her five-year marriage had ended, which left her stunned and devastated. Sarah's empathic side felt she needed to shoulder her friend's pain and support her as she navigated the tragedy of her relationship ending.

She constantly answered Rachel's phone calls to hear her vent about her ex-husband and her feelings. However, Sarah also had her own problems. Her demanding job robbed her of some family time with her kids, and her mother had recently had a stroke. Eventually, she reached a breaking point where she realized that her emotional support to Rachel had become more of a drain than a help.

She stopped picking up and returning Rachel's calls, which only compounded the agony of her friend. Rachel concluded that Sarah no longer cared about her and that they had grown apart. Sarah couldn't help but feel hurt and remorseful. She was no longer able to bear the guilt that haunted her day and night, so she expressed these feelings to me.

I explained that she wasn't being selfish or overly critical of her friend by not responding to her phone calls, and we worked together to make a plan that would better support her needs. They both agreed to discuss their issues and create healthy boundaries in their relationship. Now, it's been three years since the incident, and they have rekindled their friendship.

If you find yourself constantly helping and supporting others, you may want to look for ways to establish clear boundaries. You should also set aside some time each day to do something just for you — read a book, go for a walk, meditate — and let go of the guilt you feel from not responding to your friends and family members.

How Can Empaths Use Their Gifts to Connect with Others?

If you identify as an empath, you're already equipped with a variety of tools that can help you manage your relationships. It now boils down to how you choose to use them. Here are some suggestions that will improve your relationships with other people:

Practice Active Listening

One of the simplest yet most effective ways to connect with people is to listen to them with an open mind. We must be aware of what they are saying before judging or dismissing their feelings. It may feel awkward, especially if you're used to talking over other people, but active listening can help build trust and understanding.

Show genuine interest in what others have to say and understand their point of view, even if you disagree with them.

Set Boundaries

As an empath, it's easy to become engrossed in other people's emotions and lose sight of yours. But then, you must know how to set boundaries to protect your energy and avoid feeling overwhelmed or drained. This begins with being clear about your limits and communicating them to others. It can be as simple as saying, "I need some alone time right now," or "I'm not comfortable discussing this topic."

Use Your Intuition

Being an empath implies a strong sense of intuition, which can help you connect with people on a deeper level. So, you must trust your instincts and listen to your gut feelings. If something doesn't feel right, it probably isn't. On the other hand, if you feel drawn to someone or something, it's worth exploring that connection further.

Practice Self-Care

There is no better way to nurture others than to take care of yourself first. This is especially true when you consider that you are one person, yet you will be in charge of meeting the needs of multiple people. So, make sure to put aside some time to rest and recharge your energy. Self-care activities such as meditation, exercise, or spending time in nature will help you manage your emotions and prevent burnout.

Practice Gratitude

We may not be able to control the thoughts and feelings of others, but we can control how we react to them. One way to do this is to practice gratitude. How effective is this approach? In a study conducted by psychologist Martin Seligman, participants who practiced gratitude for one week reported higher levels of happiness and lower levels of depression. These effects lasted for up to six months.

In the context of relationships, practicing gratitude can help empaths appreciate the positive qualities and actions of others, even in difficult or challenging situations. For example, if an empath struggles to connect with a friend who is going through a tough time, they might reflect on three good things about that friend each day, such as their sense of humor, loyalty, or kindness. This can help the empath focus on the positive aspects of the relationship and build a deeper sense of appreciation and connection with their friend.

One proven exercise I share with my clients is "The Three Good Things" technique. It is a simple practice that involves reflecting on three positive things that happened each day and expressing gratitude for them. Embracing this technique will help you cultivate a greater sense of connection and empathy and, in turn, strengthen your relationships.

IN WHAT WAYS CAN EMPATHS PROTECT THEMSELVES IN RELATIONSHIPS?

Some empaths struggle to connect with others because they overthink everything and worry about how they will be perceived. It's a good idea to limit this type of overthinking by reminding yourself that the opinions of others shouldn't impact how you feel about yourself. You are not defined by the expectations and judgments of others. In fact, the way you define yourself is much more important than the opinion of others. To that end, here are some ways you can protect yourself in any relationship:

Enjoy a Healthy Life Outside of the Relationship

As an empath, it's crucial to have a life outside of your relationship that brings you joy and fulfillment. This could mean pursuing hobbies or interests you enjoy, spending time with supportive friends and family, or engaging in self-care activities that recharge your batteries. Don't spend so much time obsessing over your partner's needs that you miss out on the actions in your life. Some "me time" can help you regain clarity and lighten your mental load.

Avoid People-Pleasing or Narcissistic Traits

In my experience, many empaths have difficulty setting boundaries because they over-compensate by trying to please people, usually in an effort to feel less lonely. But pleasing others will never feel good, especially if it's done at the expense of your own feelings. This could include playing the role of a doormat and agreeing with everything others say to avoid arguments.

This trait sits well with narcissistic behavior, as it feeds off the need for approval from the next person. So, if your partner is critical and needy, you may feel the need to put up with their toxic attitude because you don't want to rock the boat. While avoiding conflict and maintaining peace can be tempting, you might wind up with resentment and eventually call it quits.

The reason for such an outcome isn't far-fetched. You've become so dependent on that person that you are less likely to stand up for yourself in critical moments. That's not a sustainable relationship. Your aim should be to spend more time in the company of those who are respectful, supportive, and empathetic toward your needs and emotions. Remember, it is always a two-way street.

CREATE A PHYSICAL SPACE FOR YOUR HYPERSENSITIVE SYSTEM TO UNFURL

Creating a physical space where you can experience your emotions without being overly affected by others is a good idea. For example, you could set up a meditation area at home or in your office, where you can retreat to when you feel overwhelmed. Alternatively, you could go to a public space like the library or a park where you can unwind for as long as you want. This will allow you to come down from high emotional intensity.

You might also try unfurling your emotional burden in front of a mirror and watch yourself as it happens. It is easy to get too caught up in what others think about you, which adds to your overwhelming emotions. But the fact that you are watching yourself decompress helps you stay focused on your feelings and sensations.

Be Aware of Your Energy and Stay Away from People who Negatively Impact Your Vibration

You might be tempted to always be around people who make you feel good. However, if you want to grow as an individual and learn more about your relationship patterns, you should strive to spend time with others who challenge you to think deeper. This way, you can learn how to handle uncomfortable situations and develop the confidence to know your limits.

Your energy can help you decide who is a positive influence in your life and who is not. For instance, if you notice a drop in your vibration the instant you enter a room, it's a red flag that you shouldn't spend time with that person.

Have Your Best Interests at Heart

You're not being selfish if you make decisions in the best interest of your health and well-being. Remember, life isn't about pleasing others; you shouldn't feel guilty about putting yourself first.

There's a good chance you'll sacrifice your own needs in the interest of helping someone else, and this isn't always a bad thing. But you shouldn't sacrifice yourself for a long time just to avoid confrontation or hurt feelings. It might feel like the right thing to do in the moment, but it will hurt both you and your partner in the long run.

The people you are close to are your responsibility and duty, and if they can't support you in making a healthy choice, they shouldn't be a part of your life.

Share Your Emotional Experience with Your Partner

We all need a shoulder to lean on at times, and sharing your feelings with others is healthy, even in romantic relationships. It can be nerve-wracking to bear the burden all by yourself. Doing so is a recipe for depression and suicidal tendencies. There is no reason to suffer in silence. Partners who share their problems and feelings are more likely to enjoy a healthy state of mind and a sense of togetherness.

I encourage my clients to share their emotional experiences with their partners. But they shouldn't expect their partners to solve the problems or to have all the answers. Remember that we are all individuals with personal views and opinions, so it's normal that the other person will need time to understand and acknowledge your perspective.

Ways to Find and Connect with Other Empaths

There are many things that empaths can do to help themselves, but connecting with others who can relate to their emotional experiences is an even better way to take care of oneself. Here are some tips on how to know someone else is an empath and how to connect with them to support your emotional wellness.

OBSERVE PEOPLE'S EMOTIONS AND BEHAVIORS

Most empaths have a strong sense of people's emotions and can pick up on subtle changes in energy. They are often attuned to other people's feelings because their energy strongly influences others. This makes it easier to spot people who share similar feelings and emotions, allowing you to connect with them on a deeper level.

However, it's important to remember that not everyone who is sensitive to emotions is an empath. For this reason, you need to approach potential connections with an open mind.

LOOK FOR EMPATH-RELATED GROUPS ONLINE

Finding people with similar interests and experiences has never been easier than with the power of the internet. Many online groups and communities are dedicated to offering support and fostering empathic connections among members. They often provide a forum for you to freely express your feelings and be educated on how to better deal with your emotional sensitivity. Some notable Facebook and web communities include Awakening Community, Empowering Empaths, and The Rising Empath.

ATTEND LOCAL EMPATH MEETUPS

Empaths can sometimes feel like the "odd one out" in their day-to-day lives because they experience feelings and emotions differently from other people. Attending local events for people like you can provide a strong sense of belonging. Some cities have local chapters that focus on supporting those with emotional sensitivities. If you can't find an existing group near you, you can host one yourself.

BE OPEN AND HONEST ABOUT YOUR EMOTIONS

It's important to remember that building a strong empathic connection with others requires vulnerability and trust. To connect with other empaths, you must be upfront about your emotions and how you perceive the world around you. You don't need to feel ashamed of your feelings and experiences. Instead, use them as a springboard to find others who can relate to your challenges and triumphs.

In summary, it is crucial for people who identify as empaths to prioritize their emotional well-being. Cultivating supportive and emotionally-healthy relationships is one effective approach towards achieving this goal.

In the meantime, you can take the first step toward connecting with others who understand your situation by taking this quiz. It takes less than 5 minutes and may provide insights into your empathic tendencies.

Self-Assessment Quiz

1. How do you typically feel in crowded places such as shopping malls or concerts?

a) Overwhelmed and drained

b) Energized and excited

c) Indifferent

2. How do you cope with other people's negative emotions?

a) I absorb them and feel them deeply

b) I try to offer solutions to make them feel better

c) I avoid those situations entirely

3. What kind of self-care practices do you find most helpful?

a) Spending time alone in nature or a quiet space

b) Engaging in social activities with friends or loved ones

c) Exercising or engaging in physical activity

4. How do you set boundaries with others?

(a) I struggle to say no and often overextend myself

b) I am assertive and clear with my boundaries

c) I avoid conflict and hope the other person will pick up on my cues

5. How do you handle your own emotions?

(a) I often feel overwhelmed by my emotions and have a hard time managing them

b) I am able to recognize and regulate my emotions effectively

c) I tend to suppress my emotions or ignore them entirely

6. How do you handle stressful or overwhelming

situations?

a) I tend to shut down or retreat from the situation

b) I actively seek out support from others

c) I try to power through and handle it on my own

7. How do you navigate difficult conversations or conflicts with others?

a) I avoid confrontation and often sacrifice my own needs to keep the peace

b) I am able to communicate assertively and work towards finding a resolution

c) I tend to get overly emotional and have a hard time communicating effectively

8. How do you handle your own personal growth and

development?

a) I am constantly seeking out new ways to improve and grow as a person

b) I tend to get overwhelmed by the process and don't know where to start

c) I don't see the need for personal growth and am content with the status quo

Scoring:

For each question, assign yourself the following points:

a) 1 point

b) 2 points

c) 0 points

Add up your points and see which category you fall under:

0-8 points: You may not identify strongly as an empath or may not have developed strong empathic abilities yet. This is not necessarily a good or bad thing, but it's important to keep in mind that empathy can be a valuable skill in many areas of life, such as building relationships and understanding others. You may want to consider exploring ways to develop your empathic abilities or focusing on other skills and strengths that come naturally to you.

8-12 points: You may struggle with setting boundaries and managing your emotions effectively. It's important to prioritize self-care and work on building a support system to help you navigate difficult situations. Consider setting aside time for yourself to recharge and engage in activities that bring you joy and relaxation. Practice saying no when you need to and communicating your needs clearly to others. Seek out support from trusted friends or professionals when needed. With some effort and practice, you can develop stronger emotional resilience and balance.

13-16 points: You have a good balance of empathy and assertiveness. Keep focusing on self-care and personal growth to continue building your resilience. Practice setting healthy boundaries with others and continue to hone your communication skills. Consider expanding your knowledge and skills in areas such as active listening, conflict resolution, and emotional regulation. Remember to prioritize your own needs and goals while also considering the needs of those around you. With continued effort and growth, you can become an even stronger empath and communicator.

A Short Message from the Author

Hi, are you enjoying the book thus far? I'd love to hear your thoughts! Many readers do not know how hard reviews are to come by, and how much they help an author.

I would be incredibly thankful if you could take just 60 seconds to write a brief review, even if it's just a few sentences!

Thank you for taking the time to share your thoughts!

Chapter 5: Understanding and Navigating Highly Sensitive People

"Highly sensitive people have a natural ability to bring depth, meaning, and beauty to the world." - Bianca Sparacino

Why do people with identical genetic information, the same upbringing, and the same family of origin grow up to have completely different outlooks on life? And why do those who grew up in the same circumstances become very different people? How is it that some people turn out to be happy and successful while others don't? To find answers to such questions, one needs to understand what makes us humans different and the importance of having a heightened state of awareness about our individual needs and preferences.

As Author Kelly Moran said, "We are all the same, and we are all different." In this chapter, we will explore the concept of high sensitivity and its impact. High sensitivity, or sensory processing sensitivity, is a trait that affects approximately 15-20% of the population. People with this quality are more aware of subtleties in their environment, have stronger emotional responses to stimuli, and may become overwhelmed by sensory input more easily than others.

This trait is not a disorder or a condition but a natural variation in how our nervous system processes information. Like most biological and psychological characteristics, it can be a strength or a challenge, depending on how it is understood and managed. When properly harnessed, it can boost self-awareness. For example, highly sensitive people can use their sensitivity to better understand and appreciate the world around them. They can make themselves aware of their needs and adapt accordingly.

How to Identify a Highly Sensitive Person in You or Someone You Know

What are some of the characteristics of a highly sensitive person? How can you identify them in yourself or someone else? Here are some cues to watch:

Sensitivity to Loud Noises or Bright Lights

When exposed to loud noises or bright lights, do you feel overwhelmed or startled easily? Is it hard for you to relax at night when there are noisy neighbors or street lights shining on your bedroom window? Sensitive people are more aware of sound, light, and other stimuli, making it difficult for them to relax when their environment becomes too loud or bright.

I have a friend whose son is highly sensitive. He often stays up late because of the noise from the garbage trucks that run midnight pickups near their home. On the other hand, his sister can sleep through a thunderstorm and, as such, hardly gets woken up by the noise at night. Despite being siblings, they are both quite different when it comes to managing their sensitivity.

BEING EASILY OVERWHELMED OR OVERSTIMULATED

Highly sensitive people react strongly to sensory information. This means that situations that others may find exciting or invigorating can be in over their heads. For example, a crowded party with loud music and lots of people may infuse anxiety and claustrophobia in them. They may feel a dire need to step away from the "madness" and find some quiet, peaceful space to take a breather.

As someone who has dealt with sensory overload before, I often found myself in over my head during annual gatherings with family and friends. Throughout the evening, I spent most of my time on the sidelines, seeking out a quiet spot to take a breather. After one of these events, a friend and I had a chat about how I was feeling and made a mental note to be more aware of my needs during future gatherings with large crowds.

A Tendency to be More Emotional and Empathetic

In the aftermath of tragic events such as 9/11, the Sandy Hook shooting, or terrorist attacks, highly sensitive people may experience a sense of powerlessness and heightened alarm. They may even be overwhelmed by an intense wave of grief or depression, which can last longer due to their deep compassion and strong emotional connections to affected individuals.

For some highly sensitive people, it's not uncommon to spend months or even years contemplating and ruminating over such events, while others may have already moved on. If you find yourself unable to move past an emotional event that has occurred in the past, it's possible that you are highly sensitive.

A Strong Need for Downtime and Alone Time

How often have you found yourself withdrawing from a situation or a person because you just wanted to be alone? Perhaps, your partner just can't fathom why you need that "me time" when everyone else is socializing. For highly sensitive people, their need for solitude is much stronger, so they might have difficulty fitting in with those who seek out social activities regularly.

A Tendency to be a Perfectionist or Highly Detail-Oriented

This is one of the most difficult characteristics for others to understand. Because highly sensitive people are often very detail-oriented, they may obsess over the smallest details of a task or project that might leave anyone else feeling frustrated and agitated. This tendency may stem from an over-active imagination that leads to endless brainstorming about all the ways things could go wrong or how better things could be if only they do this or that.

This quality can become a self-defeating behavior if it goes unchecked. Highly sensitive people may spend more time planning, checking over and over their work, and fretting over how others will react. They may be perceived as overly serious, critical, and uptight, which will lead to further isolation.

POTENTIAL BENEFITS AND CHALLENGES OF BEING AN HSP

There are perks and challenges to being highly sensitive. Some of the potential benefits include the following:

HEIGHTENED AWARENESS OF ONE'S SURROUNDINGS

As highly sensitive people are often more observant than others, they are often better able to notice things others may overlook. This may include small details in nature, subtle changes in facial expression, or subtle changes in body language. This heightened awareness also makes them more attuned to their own body signals.

Strong Empathy and Emotional Intelligence

Being highly sensitive can contribute to a person's empathy and emotional intelligence. Most HSPs deeply understand how their words or actions affect others, and this sensitivity helps them to better empathize and connect with people on a more emotional level. They naturally make excellent listeners, compassionate friends, and effective communicators.

A Deep Appreciation for Art, Music, and Nature

Another hallmark of highly sensitive people is their ability to appreciate and be deeply moved by the beauty and intricacy of nature and various forms of art. A highly sensitive person might experience a profound sense of wonder when listening to music or gazing upon a painting. They may be more inclined to seek out natural settings such as parks, forests, or beaches for relaxation, renewal, and inspiration.

STRONG INTUITION AND THE ABILITY TO READ OTHERS WELL

Highly sensitive people have strong intuition and are skilled at reading others based on subtle cues like body language or tone of voice. They tend to be perceptive and excellent judges of character. This ability helps them navigate social situations and build successful relationships.

On the other hand, some of the challenges of being an HSP include the following:

EASILY OVERWHELMED AND OVERSTIMULATED

High sensitivity to light, noise, touch, and other stimuli can often result in overwhelming feelings and irritation, especially when it is unexpected. HSPs may even experience panic attacks in specific situations, such as a loud concert or a thunderstorm. Sensory overload makes it difficult to focus on activities, stay motivated, and complete tasks on time.

Struggles with Anxiety and Stress

Strong reactions to events or situations can result in heightened levels of stress, anxiety, and fear. As a highly sensitive person, you may be more prone to internalizing negative experiences and emotions and, as a result, become depressed, irritated, and exhausted. In addition, you may experience sleep disturbances, such as restlessness and insomnia.

A Tendency to Take Things Personally and be Overly Self-Critical

It comes as no surprise that HSPs are also highly self-critical. Their heightened awareness and sensitivity makes them more conscious of criticisms and judgments, which may lead to extreme self-criticism. Many HSPs experience perfectionist tendencies that lead them to put unnecessary pressure on themselves and push themselves to the limits.

Struggles with Close Relations

While being highly s...
empathy, compassio...
others on an emotic...
challenges in social si...
find yourself second-...
feelings or criticizing o... ..., which can lead to social anxiety and isolation.

Strategies for Coping with High Sensitivity

If you are a highly sensitive person, there are several coping mechanisms you can employ.

- Create a serene and visually toned-down environment (maybe a dedicated room in your home) to reduce overstimulation and promote relaxation.

specific time intervals of the day ... your batteries which will improve mental clarity and mood.

- Set healthy boundaries to prevent overcommitment and becoming overwhelmed.
- Practice regular self-care activities such as meditation, yoga, and deep breathing to reduce stress and promote well-being
- Have a support system of understanding friends and family members. You can also join a support group or consult a therapist.

IMPORTANCE OF SELF-CARE FOR HSPs

Self-care is essential for highly sensitive people as it helps to manage the unique challenges associated with their sensitivity. Here are some reasons you should embrace this technique:

HELPS TO MANAGE OVERSTIMULATION

HSPs' biological composition predisposes them to be overwhelmed by external stimuli. However, self-care practices such as meditation, mindfulness, and journalling can help to reduce overstimulation and prevent stress and anxiety.

Improves Emotional Regulation

External stimuli, whether positive or negative, can significantly affect an HSP's emotional state. While it is impossible to control external stimuli, self-care strategies can teach HSPs how to identify sources of emotional stress and work through them. This way, they can manage their emotional responses and better cope with external events.

Builds Resilience

Highly sensitive people may face unique challenges related to their sensitivity, such as criticism, rejection, or feeling misunderstood. Engaging in self-care activities, such as exercise, healthy eating, or maintaining healthy relationships, can help to cultivate a stronger sense of self and improve overall well-being.

NAVIGATING RELATIONSHIPS AS AN HSP

You may find it challenging to establish firm boundaries, communicate your needs and emotions effectively, or handle intense feelings from your spouse, colleagues, or family members. Here are some practical suggestions to assist you in overcoming these obstacles:

PRACTICE SELF LOVE

There is no better way to find true happiness and fulfillment than to love yourself. It's natural for you to shoulder everyone's burden, but this shouldn't come at the price of your physical and mental health or your needs. Besides, you need to be in a state of balance to give that kind of support.

One way to build up that reserve is to give yourself the love and attention you deserve. You may then give freely and joyfully contribute to others without jeopardizing your needs.

STAND UP FOR YOURSELF

When things get out of hand, and there is not enough time to deal with everything on your own, stand up for yourself. Speak to people calmly and assertively, and make your point loud and clear. HSPs generally avoid conflict because of the discomfort and guilt it can trigger. They would rather take all the blame, even when they aren't at fault. This puts them in a vulnerable position that isn't healthy for them or the relationship.

That is why it's important to develop healthy conflict-resolution skills. If you find yourself in a heated situation, take a deep breath and say: "I need to step away for a while so I can reflect on this," and then give yourself some time to calm down.

BEWARE OF PREDATORS

Just because a person is good-looking and charismatic doesn't mean they are worthy of your time. Some may try to drain you of your energy and resources, expecting you to solve all their problems without adding any value to your life. If your relationship is draining and you feel used, it's probably time to move on and find someone who will genuinely support and help you. Always ask yourself: "Are they bringing out the best in me?" If the answer is a big fat no, it's probably time to re-evaluate the relationship.

Don't Always Play the Hero

Sometimes we can fall into the trap of always trying to be the hero, especially if we're highly sensitive people. We want to fix everything and make everyone happy, which can lead us down the wrong path. If we're in an unhappy marriage or a loveless relationship, it could be because we've taken on too much responsibility for our partner's problems or our children's issues.

Even when we have good intentions and know what's best for others, it can backfire if they feel like we're trying to control or intrude. The truth is, we can't rescue other people from their struggles. They need to learn and grow on their own, and sometimes that means we have to step back and let them figure things out for themselves. Of course, we should always show compassion and support, but we shouldn't take on their burdens.

Accept Yourself

If you don't appreciate your sensitivity, it's unlikely that the next person will. Once you accept and embrace who you are, finding someone who appreciates your unique qualities will be easier. We often tend to be overly self-critical and put ourselves down because we think we should be better than we currently are.

While self-improvement is important, it's crucial not to try and change our personality and give up the things that make us special just to please others. If someone belittles or criticizes you because you are a highly sensitive person, it is a reflection of their own issues. You don't need someone like that in your life.

In summary, high sensitivity has its merits and demerits, but with the right strategies and support, you can thrive and succeed in all aspects of life. It begins with identifying the specific indicators of this trait, practicing self-care, promoting self-worth, setting healthy boundaries, and seeking support when needed. When all that is in place, you can easily navigate relationships, work, and life with confidence and resilience.

Chapter 6: Empaths in Society and Culture

"Empathy is the key to humanizing the world and bringing us closer together." - Simon Sinek

Empathy is the bedrock of intimacy and close connections; in its absence, relationships remain emotionally shallow. Empathy has helped us build and maintain societies and cultures over time. For empaths, it's like they have a special superpower. They just get people and can relate to what others are feeling emotionally.

But being an empath in today's world isn't always a walk in the park. It can be tough to handle your emotions and boundaries when constantly bombarded with everyone else's feelings. Furthermore, some people may try to exploit an empath's sensitivity for their own gain.

Empathy is starting to get the recognition it deserves in our culture. More and more people are seeing how important it is to build healthy relationships, both personally and professionally. That's where empaths can shine, especially in fields like counseling, therapy, and social work.

It's not all sunshine and rainbows, though. Society still puts a lot of value on traits like being assertive, competitive, and independent. That can make it hard for empaths to thrive and be appreciated for what they bring to the table. Sometimes they get labeled as weak or too emotional, which is unfair.

But here's the thing, empaths have a lot to offer. They can help build a more compassionate and inclusive world. An empathic leader can create a workplace culture where people feel understood and valued, while an empathic artist can use their craft to inspire social change.

Being an empath is quite complex and multi-layered. There are ups and downs, challenges, and advantages. However, if empaths can embrace and use their abilities to promote empathy and understanding, they can significantly impact the world around them.

In this chapter, we'll explore the roles and impact of empathy, how empaths can positively influence society, and some potential challenges they may face in our fast-paced world.

THE ROLE OF EMPATHS IN DIFFERENT CULTURES AND SOCIETIES THROUGHOUT HISTORY

Throughout history, empaths have been recognized for their ability to sense and understand the emotions and experiences of others. In some cultures, this ability was viewed as a gift that was passed down from generation to generation, ensuring that the individual who wielded it had a significant and influential role in that society. Many empaths were revered as spiritual leaders, healers, and oracles. They were thought to possess supernatural powers and communicate with spirits to provide guidance and protect their communities from attacks and diseases.

A notable example of empaths in ancient Egypt were the priestesses of the goddess Hathor, who were believed to have the ability to heal and provide guidance to those who sought their help. They would use their empathic abilities to connect with the divine and offer counsel and support. This wasn't strange, as Hathor was a goddess associated with many things, including love, fertility, and motherhood. She was often depicted as a cow, a symbol of fertility and nurturing, and her temples were centers of healing and rejuvenation.

The ancient Egyptian medical texts known as the Ebers Papyrus and the Edwin Smith Papyrus both contain references to the healing abilities of the priestesses of Hathor. They describe various medical treatments and procedures, including the use of medicinal plants and herbs, surgery, and magical spells, all of which were believed to have been taught to them by the goddess herself.

In Japan, the term "Kanjo Hyakubai" translates to "reading emotions in one hundred ways." It refers to the ability to perceive and understand the emotions of others through subtle facial expressions, gestures, and tone of voice. This ability is highly valued in Japanese culture, as it is believed to promote harmonious relationships and social cohesion.

The ancient Greeks also recognized the importance of empaths. In Ancient Greek mythology, Hermes was one of the most famous empaths. He was the god of swift travel and communication and was also regarded as the messenger of the gods. As such, he was associated with healing and prophecy, and was also said to have the power to change his form at will, a skill which allowed him to walk between realms and interact with the spirits.

In Hinduism, empaths are recognized as having a deep

understanding of the nature of the universe and are considered to be on a path to enlightenment. This is because empathy is seen as an essential quality for spiritual growth and development. By cultivating empathy, one can understand the interconnectedness of all beings and develop a deeper sense of compassion and love for all.

The concept of "Karuna" is a central tenet of Hinduism. Karuna refers to the ability to empathize with the suffering of others and to work towards alleviating that suffering through compassionate action. It is a fundamental principle in many Hindu traditions, including yoga and meditation. It is often seen as an extension of the concept of ahimsa, which means non-violence or non-harming.

By practicing ahimsa, one seeks to avoid causing harm to others or oneself. Karuna takes this one step further by actively seeking to alleviate the suffering of others. The ultimate goal of this spiritual practice in Hinduism is to achieve enlightenment, which is the state of ultimate realization of the true nature of the universe. Empathy and compassion are essential qualities for achieving this goal, as they help cultivate a sense of oneness with all beings.

In many African cultures, empaths are respected and revered as diviners or seers who possess the ability to communicate with the spirits and ancestors. Diviners are believed to be able to use their heightened intuition and empathic abilities to access the spiritual realm and receive guidance and messages from ancestors, deities, or other spiritual entities.

The role of diviners varies from one culture to another, but they often play a crucial role in providing guidance, healing, and protection to members of their communities. They may offer advice on various aspects of life, such as health, relationships, and decision-making. They may also use divination tools like bones, shells, or cards to help them access the spiritual realm and interpret messages.

Diviners are accountable for using their abilities for the greater good of their community. Their empathic powers and spiritual connections are intended to promote healing, justice, and peace. They may also collaborate with other healers and practitioners, such as herbalists or traditional physicians, to provide their clients with holistic healing. In some West African cultures, those who communicate with the spirits of the dead are known as "Djembes." Many of them fall into the category of empaths.

Empaths also played a vital role in medieval Europe, particularly during the Black Death pandemic. Some empaths, referred to as "plague saints," were believed to be able to heal the sick and protect people from the disease. Many people turned to these empaths for help and guidance during the pandemic, and their empathic abilities were often seen as evidence of their divine connection.

The traditional Native American societies held a similar belief in the power of empaths, who they referred to as "Heyokas." They were believed to have the ability to transform negative energy into positive energy through their empathic abilities. Heyokas would often perform rituals and ceremonies to help members of their community deal with emotional pain and trauma.

In modern times, empaths are recognized for their ability to provide support and guidance to others. They are often employed in caring professions such as nursing, social work, and counseling, where their ability to empathize with clients can be valuable. They've also played a significant role in literature and the arts.

Many writers, poets, and artists have been recognized for their ability to capture and convey the emotions of others. For example, Emily Dickinson is often considered to be an empath, as her poetry often reflects a deep understanding of the human experience. The influence of empaths is seen in social justice movements, given that empathy is an essential component of understanding and combating systemic oppression and inequality.

For example, during the Civil Rights Movement in the United States, many white allies who supported the movement were empaths who could empathize with the experiences of Black Americans and understand the pain and trauma caused by racism. It is without a doubt that the increasing awareness and understanding of empathy and emotional intelligence will lead to a greater appreciation and value for empaths in various fields.

We may see more empaths become valuable contributors to creating more compassionate and understanding workplaces, communities, and institutions.

THE IMPACT OF EMPATHS ON SOCIETY AND CULTURE

The empathic ability to connect with others, understand and care for their well-being, and act with compassion is a vital component of our social fabric. This means that we play a crucial role in shaping our society and culture by virtue of our innate sensitivity and love for humanity. This core attribute of our identity influences our thoughts, behaviors, and practices and contributes to the formation of a cohesive and compassionate community.

To this end, our impact on society and culture cannot

be overstated, as we bring unique perspectives and values promoting empathy, understanding, and cooperation. There is no question that when a group of empathic people comes together, the energy generated can have an enormous impact on the world. So far, we have seen convincing evidence of this in many areas of human endeavor.

A notable example that demonstrates how an empath can influence society at large is the work of Mahatma Gandhi. While the political leader was known for his non-violent civil disobedience movement against the British colonial government, his empathy, love, and compassion were a central part of his movement, which helped unite people in India in their struggle for independence from British colonialism.

Mahatma Gandhi connected with people from all walks of life, understood their struggles and aspirations, and inspired them to act with compassion and nonviolence. His philosophy of nonviolent resistance influenced the civil rights movement in the United States and other struggles for social justice around the world.

Another example is the work of Mother Teresa, who devoted her life to caring for the sick and poor in India and other parts of the world. She exemplified the power of empathy and compassion to transform individual lives and communities. Her selfless service inspired millions and led to the establishment of the Missionaries of Charity, a global organization dedicated to helping the needy.

The impact of empaths is also perceptible in medical sciences, with the mental health sector being a prime example. Empathic psychologists and counselors are more inclined to relate to patients on an empathic level and provide tailored treatment and guidance that produce positive long-term results. Their in-depth knowledge of mind-body connection and innate empathetic traits are instrumental to advancing therapeutic techniques, such as cognitive-behavioral therapy (CBT) and mindfulness-based interventions.

Empaths are also valuable assets in the business world, particularly in companies that prioritize customer satisfaction. They can read customers' emotions and needs, enabling them to provide personalized and effective customer service. An empathetic salesperson may better understand a customer's needs and make appropriate product recommendations, leading to higher sales and customer loyalty. Additionally, empathetic leadership has been linked to higher employee morale and job satisfaction, resulting in a more positive work environment and increased productivity.

The arts and entertainment industries also benefit from empathic individuals' transformative power. Many successful musicians, writers, and actors have been identified as empaths, and their ability to tap into the emotions of their audience has led to some of the most moving and impactful works of art. For example, Adele's music is known for its emotional depth and resonance, directly resulting from her empathetic nature.

Finally, we've witnessed the cruciality of empathy in social justice movements, which stems from a place of compassion and understanding for human rights and freedom. Many artists, activists, and social entrepreneurs worldwide have used their voices and platforms to decry all forms of oppression, abuse, stigma, and discrimination while inspiring social change. Their insights have been instrumental in shaping more inclusive and equitable policies.

During the civil rights movement, empathetic leaders such as Martin Luther King Jr. used their ability to understand the emotions of both the oppressed and the oppressor to foster dialogue and promote peaceful change. All these notable accomplishments and more are a direct pointer to how influential empaths are on society and culture in various fields. So, as we continue to enjoy the benefits and results of empathy, we must recognize and value the efforts of their contributors toward human progress.

WHAT POTENTIAL CHALLENGES DO EMPATHS FACE IN OUR FAST-PACED WORLD?

While the empath's contributions to society and culture can yield positive outcomes, they often come at a cost. Our sense of duty, compassion, and care can overwhelm our empathy, leading to burnout and personal suffering if not managed appropriately. Moreover, it is possible to become so invested in everything else that we neglect our own emotional needs and well-being. Some of the challenges linked to empaths making a positive impact on society include the following:

Emotional Overload

Empaths are "emotional sponges" that absorb other people's feelings, moods, and energies. However, constant exposure to strong emotions without a way to recharge can make them lose energy and focus over time. This impairs their ability to function optimally in fields that require a high level of emotional engagement.

Difficulty with Delegation

Not everyone is equipped to perform tasks that do not come naturally to them. And since empaths are natural helpers and have the desire to contribute, it may be difficult for them to pass off tasks, even when they don't appeal to their natural strengths. As a result, they over-commit themselves to work and end up burned out. This was formerly the case for some of my clients, particularly those who struggled to work effectively as a team to increase productivity.

Balancing Self-Care and Service

There is a time for everything, and prioritizing self-care over service is essential to a balanced, fulfilled life. The empath's unique sensitivity, combined with a strong sense of compassion and duty, can make it challenging to maintain equilibrium and prevent energy drain. In most cases, they bury themselves in their work, sacrificing their personal life in the process. Their inability to take time off is rooted in their sense of guilt over the abandonment of their service to mankind. However, failure to schedule time to recharge will result in exhaustion, mental breakdown, low productivity, and even illness.

Boundaries

Overcommitment to work and other people's needs can lead to an all-or-nothing approach to life. Empaths dedicate their time and energy to those in need, which is admirable. But then, the inability to say no, even when the situation is detrimental to their well-being, can lead to resentment and frustration. It undermines their ability to perform at optimum levels in all areas of their lives.

In conclusion, a society in which empaths are able to channel their energy, compassion, and care toward positive endeavors that are aligned with their natural strengths can be a boon to humanity. However, it will require a deep understanding of the work environment and the personal needs and challenges of the empath to make it work.

As a clarion call to those gifted with empathic abilities, it is crucial to manage and cultivate these qualities while balancing them with the need to recharge. That way, you can make significant contributions to society without losing yourself in the process.

Chapter 7: Navigating Challenges and Harnessing the Strengths and Gifts of Emotional Sensitivity

"Highly sensitive people are not weak or fragile, we are simply more attuned to the world around us." - Susan Cain

"How do you make changes for yourself and others?" It's a compelling question that can feel personal for many and, at times, overwhelming. Empathic individuals may particularly resonate with its complexity and emotional depth. Emotional sensitivity is vital to our social and personal well-being. But, as with any unique trait, it can be difficult to know how to navigate its challenges and create changes when you're struggling to feel at ease in your own skin.

At its best, the experience of being an empath is a powerful learning tool that can transform your perspective, sense of self, and actions. But it can also be a burden, a force that can take over and cause you to feel lost, anxious, depressed, or out of control. That's why it's essential to learn how to balance what you are feeling with what you are doing, a skill we cover in depth in this book.

WHAT STRATEGIES WORK BEST TO MANAGE THE UNIQUE CHALLENGES OF EMPATHS AND HSPS?

As I mentioned in the introduction, empathy and sensitivity can be both a blessing and a burden, which I liken to a rose with thorns or Superman with kryptonite. This means that as much as your gifts benefit humanity, they come with their set of challenges that can negatively impact your overall well-being if not properly managed. For this reason, you need to be armed to the teeth with all the resources necessary to address them.

Fortunately, many resources are available to support the empath in all areas of their life, from improving self-confidence and reducing stress to creating a career that harnesses their emotional talents. Here are some of them:

Embrace Self-Care

I have discussed this on more than one occasion, but it's still worth mentioning as it is the core of your functionality. When you are constantly in other people's shoes, it can leave you drained and exhausted without enough energy to focus on yourself. The tendency is to burn the candle at both ends to continue contributing to the community. However, that would inevitably lead to your well-being coming second, with potentially devastating effects.

The first step towards managing your sensitivity and staying healthy is taking good care of yourself. I consider self-care as the foundation of the path to success. Here are some key things you can do to stay healthy as an empath:

- Eat healthy, natural foods, including lots of fruits and vegetables, whole grains, and lean protein sources.
- Limit intake of alcohol and caffeine, as they can be stimulants and interfere with sleep.
- Try to get regular and restorative sleep, which will help you stay mentally and physically fit.
- Exercise regularly, preferably in nature or in an outdoor setting.
- Participate in physical activities that you enjoy, such as running, yoga, or rock climbing.
- Practice deep breathing techniques, meditation, or mindfulness exercises to reduce stress and cultivate self-awareness.
- Limit screen time, including television, smartphones, and computers, to increase the time you spend doing things you enjoy.

- Engage in creative outlets, such as painting, drawing, dancing, writing, or singing, to help release pent-up emotions and express yourself in a healthy manner.
- Use the power of visualization to achieve your goals.
- Practice self-forgiveness and forgiveness of others, as it helps to reduce anger, frustration, and resentment that can lead to physical illnesses.

IDENTIFY YOUR TRIGGERS

As empaths, we tend to have very strong emotions, which means that we can get triggered and taken over when we sense any negative energy. For example, when you see a stranger drive aggressively and you experience a strong feeling of distress, that's a clear sign that you're emotionally triggered. You need to take a deep breath and stay calm (not indifferent).

Your initial response is a perfectly normal physical reaction, but if it happens too often, it can negatively impact your physical, mental, and emotional well-being. If left unchecked, your heart rate and blood pressure will likely spike, making you more prone to anxiety and stress.

The next step is to identify the sources of these triggers and make it a point to avoid them whenever possible. It is important to note that it is nearly impossible to entirely avoid stressful situations and circumstances, which is why it is imperative that you do everything in your power to reduce your exposure to them.

Find out what pushes your emotional buttons so that you can practice self-care when these triggers occur. This may require you to be mindful of your environment, which includes the people with whom you interact and the products you use, as well as your own inner dialogue and feelings.

Finally, identify people who have power over you and distance yourself from them. For example, if a colleague constantly bullies you, report the issue; if you find large crowds overwhelming, attend events during off-peak hours or choose to go to events with a close friend who understands your sensitivity.

Plan Ahead

"What's a goal without a plan?" A wish! Just because you are an empath, it doesn't mean you can fly by the seat of your pants. It may feel exciting and adventurous initially, but it can be taxing in the long run. The key is to be organized. Set realistic goals on what type and how much value you wish to contribute, when to decompress, and what steps you can take to make them happen.

For example, you can make a list of people and situations that stress you out and decide how much time you'll spend dealing with them.

Value Your Gifts

Your worth is not determined by how you measure up to others. Rather, it's based on your own sense of self and the inherent value you place on your talents and abilities. While it is crucial to learn from your mistakes and grow from them, it's equally important to acknowledge the positive impact your gifts have made in your life and on others.

What are your gifts? I've already mentioned them in Chapter 2: high emotional intelligence, intuition, creativity, understanding others' emotions, and more. As an empath, your unique qualities can be put to good use in various industries, such as health care, business, public service, education, entertainment, and many more.

Just ensure you do your homework first and have a plan before launching any new project. There's no need to go into something without any preparation or planning. As you take a step back to discover and nurture your innate talents, use the following steps to help make your career and personal goals a reality:

- Create a "life map"
- Identify people who can assist you in reaching your goals
- Use your strengths to your advantage and build on your weaknesses
- Create a positive and realistic image of yourself
- Spend your time wisely

How to Deal with Difficult People and Insensitive Comments

Have you ever had someone tell you to "lighten up" or call you "too sensitive" when you expressed your emotional reaction? What about someone criticizing your creative ideas as too "dramatic" or "outlandish"? I'm sure it's happened to all of us at some point in our lives. These are classic examples of insensitive people who pass remarks that create self-doubt and affect our self-worth. Empaths are particularly susceptible to being hurt by them.

The key to managing these people and situations is first accepting who you are and that your sensitivity is not a weakness but a strength. Your feelings are valid, and it's absolutely okay to express them. You shouldn't let others tell you what to do or try to change you. You should also realize that you have the power to choose who you allow in your life. Just because someone is close to you doesn't mean they should be able to do as they please without you expressing your feelings.

You have the right to protect yourself from the unnecessary stress, drama, and discomfort that comes with those who tend to be inconsiderate or judgmental. Your responsibility as an empath is to speak up when you feel uncomfortable or mistreated. If you allow others to take advantage of your kindness and do as they please, you will become resentful, hurt, and angry. Here are some other helpful tips:

- Dispel their negative energy with optimism
- Set healthy boundaries and know when to call time off
- Stand up for yourself and correct the person
- Ignore the remarks (Don't take it personally)
- Tone down your emotional response

These strategies can help you navigate through the ups and downs of working with insensitive people. Remember, the world needs your gifts and talents, but that does not mean you should put yourself at risk to make it happen. It's okay to ask for what you want and need, but do it respectfully.

Should You Find a Supportive Community?

I know it can be difficult to make the time and effort to cultivate and maintain friendships when your energy is already drained from overexposure to negative emotions. However, it's essential to surround yourself with positive people who understand your sensitivity and are willing to offer their support.

One way to do that is to get involved in activities that bring you joy and help you make a positive impact. This includes volunteering, attending networking events, doing something creative, and joining or starting a group of like-minded individuals. By doing so, you'll find that you're not alone in the world and that there are others out there who are willing to share their experiences and wisdom.

I'm a firm believer that no person is an island. No matter how strong we are, we need others to help us along our path. Your best bet is to search online for communities within your local area or create one using social media. Even if you only meet one or two people who can provide you with encouragement and support, it will make a massive difference in your life.

How You Can Embrace and Develop Your Empathic Abilities

Many people are skeptical when they hear about being empathic because they associate the term with divination, fortune telling, and other "spooky" things. However, being empathic is nothing more than our innate ability to feel others' emotions and understand what they're going through. It's a natural gift that empowers you to make positive changes in the world, and it should be used to help others and not harm them.

Empaths are not weak, defective, broken, or anything else negative. Empathy is an integral part of our humanity. It's one of the greatest gifts you can ever receive. It has allowed me to tap into a deep well of wisdom and understanding of myself and others. So, I believe that everyone should cultivate their empathetic abilities as they help us see the world through the eyes of others, which ultimately makes us better persons.

Here are some tried-and-true methods that I and other successful empaths have used to embrace and develop our gifts in the past and which I believe will work for you.

- Recognize and challenge your biases, which can influence your thoughts and attitudes toward others. By being aware of them, you can work towards overcoming them and becoming more open-minded.
- Practice active listening, focusing on the speaker without interrupting or offering unsolicited advice. This allows you to understand their perspective and builds trust and respect in your relationship.
- Use thoughtful and empathetic questioning to understand the emotions and experiences of others rather than simply seeking information or solutions.
- Seek out diverse perspectives and experiences by socializing and working with people from

different backgrounds. Cultivate an attitude of non-judgment and acceptance, recognizing the richness that diversity brings.

- Nurture your curiosity about the world and the people in it, recognizing that there is always more to learn and discover. This helps to expand your understanding and empathy towards others.
- Practice emotional intelligence by being aware of your own emotions and how they may affect your interactions with others. This allows you to relate to others more effectively and build deeper connections.

WAYS TO ENCOURAGE AND EMPOWER EMPATHS AND HSPs TO ACCEPT AND HARNESS THEIR TRAITS

As you've learned in this book, empaths, and highly sensitive people are more than just sensitive and intuitive. Our unique traits allow us to build a stronger connection with others, which also means we can play a key role in improving our society and how it functions with the right support, knowledge, and attitude.

But not all empaths recognize or appreciate their sensitivity. And those who do sometimes struggle to manage the challenges it presents, so it's our responsibility as empaths to educate others and show them how they can use their abilities to improve our society. We can do that by:

Encouraging Self-Care and Self-Compassion

Empaths and HSPs need time alone to recharge and process their emotions. Encouraging them to prioritize self-care and to be gentle with themselves can help to reduce stress and overwhelm.

Providing Validation and Support

Many empaths and HSPs may feel misunderstood or excluded from groups of people who aren't as sensitive. Encouragement to seek out like-minded persons, as well as validation and support, might help them feel more understood and accepted.

Offering Coping Strategies

Not all moments are easy for empaths and HSPs, so a list of effective coping strategies can help them navigate through challenging situations and manage their reaction. They include meditation, mindfulness, and grounding techniques. These techniques are known to reduce anxiety and overstimulation.

Helping Them to See Their Strengths

While empaths and HSPs may feel overwhelmed by the challenges that come with their sensitivity, it's important to point out their strengths and qualities that they should embrace rather than shy away from. Doing this may encourage them to feel more positive about their differences.

Exercises for Empaths / Sensitive People

Meditation

- Find a quiet, comfortable place to sit or lie down.
- Set a timer for 5-10 minutes to start.
- Close your eyes or focus on a point in front of you.
- Take a few deep breaths and release any tension in your body.
- Focus on the sensation of the breath moving in and out of your body.
- If your mind wanders, gently bring your attention back to the breath.
- When the timer goes off, take a few more deep breaths before opening your eyes.

Journaling

- Set aside 10-15 minutes each day for journaling.
- Find a quiet, comfortable place to sit.

- Write down your thoughts and emotions without judgment.
- If you're not sure what to write about, start with a prompt like "Today I am feeling…"
- Write until the time is up or until you feel like you've processed what you need to.

Mindful Breathing

- Find a comfortable place to sit or lie down where you won't be disturbed for a few minutes.
- Take a few deep breaths to settle in and release any tension in your body.
- Begin to focus on your breath, noticing the sensation of the air moving in and out of your nostrils.
- As you inhale, imagine that you're inhaling positive energy and light into your body. Visualize this energy spreading throughout your body, filling you with light and positivity.
- As you exhale, imagine that you're releasing any negative energy, stress, or tension from your body. Visualize this energy leaving your

body as you exhale, and imagine that it's being transformed into positive energy as it leaves.
- Continue this pattern of inhaling positive energy and exhaling negative energy for a few minutes.
- If your mind starts to wander, gently bring your attention back to the breath and the visualization.
- When you're ready to finish the exercise, take a few more deep breaths and thank yourself for taking the time to practice self-care.

VISUALIZATION

- Find a quiet, comfortable place where you won't be disturbed for a few minutes.
- Take a few deep breaths to settle in and release any tension in your body.
- Close your eyes and visualize yourself in a peaceful, relaxing setting. This could be a beach, a forest, a meadow, or any other location that feels soothing to you.
- Notice the details of your surroundings - the colors, textures, sounds, and smells.

- Imagine that you're surrounded by a warm, glowing light that's enveloping you in a sense of peace and calm.
- Visualize yourself moving through this environment, feeling completely relaxed and at ease.
- If your mind wanders, gently bring your attention back to the visualization.
- When you're ready to finish the exercise, take a few more deep breaths and remind yourself that you can return to this peaceful state whenever you need to.

Setting Boundaries

- Identify areas of your life where you feel overwhelmed or drained.
- Determine what your limits are in those areas (e.g., how much time or energy you can realistically give).
- Practice saying "no" to requests that exceed your limits.
- Communicate your boundaries to others in a clear but compassionate way.

Conclusion

Congratulations on reaching the end of this book. You have taken an important step towards discovering and understanding the unique gifts and challenges of being an empath or highly sensitive person. You have also gained valuable insights into how you can harness your strengths and embrace your sensitivity to create a more compassionate and understanding world.

We've learned that empathy is at the heart of human connection and relationships. It allows us to understand, relate to, and accept others, regardless of their strengths and weaknesses. However, in a society where we are increasingly becoming disconnected and more self-focused, empathy has become less common in our daily lives.

Therefore, we must connect back to our empathic nature and harness its potential for building a better, more compassionate society. It begins with understanding what empathy is and how we can be more empathic towards ourselves and others. But the journey doesn't end there - empathy goes beyond understanding and extends to action.

In chapter one, we introduced the concept of empathy and emotional sensitivity, defining who an empath and highly sensitive person were. Based on the definitions provided, we understood that empaths are individuals who are highly attuned to the emotions and energy of others. They have the ability to perceive other people's thoughts and feelings based on physical cues, intuition, and imagination, making it easier to understand and help them.

Highly Sensitive People have a heightened sensitivity to their environment, including stimuli such as noise, light, and smells. They may also be sensitive to other people's emotions. We also examined their characteristics and differences before delving into the neuroscience and biology behind each trait. Notable areas of discussion included the mirror neuron system, limbic system, prefrontal cortex, hormonal factors, nervous system, and genetics.

Another aspect we discussed was the genetic and environmental factors that affect empathetic and sensitivity traits. We highlighted heritability, candidate genes, parenting style, childhood experiences, socialization, and life experiences.

Chapter two delved into the science behind empathy and how it affects our brains and bodies. We learned that empathy is not just a feeling but a physiological response that impacts our mental and physical health. We learned about empaths' unique abilities and talents, like creativity, empathy, intuition, healing, and emotional intelligence. Notable empaths discussed included Carl Jung, John Lennon, and Nelson Mandela. Of course, we couldn't pass up on uncovering the role of empathy and sensitivity in leadership and relationships.

Chapter three focused on determining if you are an empath, knowing the techniques for managing and regulating empathy, the importance of self-care, and the roles empaths play in society, among others. Each section came with proven tips and strategies that would help to boost your understanding and awareness of empathy.

With a firm grasp of empathy and sensitivity, it was time to look at "Navigating Relationships as an Empath" in chapter four. We covered common relationship dynamics that empaths may struggle with, such as codependency and toxic relationships, and also strategies for developing healthy communication skills and building strong relationships.

In chapter five, we focused on highly sensitive people: how to tell if you or someone you know falls into this category, the benefits and challenges you or that person will likely face, ideal strategies that can help you, why you should prioritize self-care, and how sensitivity can affect your work and relationships.

Chapter six reawakened our interest in the historical and cultural relevance of empathy, dating back to ancient Egypt and Greece. We also studied the present socioeconomic and cultural aspects influencing empaths. Another important consideration was the possible issues that empaths may experience in our fast-paced environment, such as trouble with delegating, emotional overload, and an imbalance between self-care and service, among other things.

In chapter seven, we learned how to navigate challenges and harness the strengths and gifts of emotional sensitivity. No stone was left unturned on other key topics, such as how to deal with difficult people and insensitive comments, the approach to finding a community of supportive empaths, how to embrace and develop your empathic abilities, and ways to encourage and empower empaths and highly sensitive people to embrace and harness their traits. This chapter also featured exercises to help your mind and body become more productive.

As we conclude this journey together, I want to leave you with a few final thoughts and inspirations.

Firstly, I want to remind you that you are not alone. Empaths and highly sensitive people have been around for centuries, and there are millions of people just like you who experience life in a deeply emotional and intuitive way. Remember that your sensitivity is not a weakness, but rather a superpower that allows you to connect with others on a profound level.

Secondly, I want to encourage you to embrace your uniqueness. The world needs more empathic and sensitive individuals who can bring compassion, understanding, and positive change to society. It is important to honor and respect your sensitivity, and to use it as a tool to help you navigate your relationships, career, and personal growth.

Thirdly, I want to remind you that self-care is critical. Being an empath or highly sensitive person can be emotionally draining, so it is essential to prioritize your mental, emotional, and physical health. Make sure to take time for yourself, set healthy boundaries, and surround yourself with supportive people who understand and appreciate your sensitivity.

Lastly, I want to encourage you to share your gifts with the world. Whether you are an artist, writer, musician, or social worker, there are endless opportunities to use your sensitivity to make a positive impact. By sharing your unique perspective and talents, you can inspire and empower others to embrace their sensitivity and make a difference in the world.

In closing, I want to thank you for taking this journey with me. I hope that this book has inspired you, given you new insights, and helped you to see your sensitivity in a positive light. Remember that being an empath or highly sensitive person is a gift, and you have the power to use your sensitivity to make the world a better place.

With love and appreciation,

Richard Banks

One more thing!

If you enjoyed this book and found it helpful, I'd be very grateful if you'd post a short review on Amazon. Your support does make a difference, and I read all the reviews personally so I can get your feedback and make this book even better. I love hearing from my readers, and I'd really appreciate it if you leave your honest feedback.

Thank you for reading!

BONUS CHAPTER

I would like to share a sneak peek into another one of my books that I think you will enjoy. The book is titled ***"THE ART OF BEING YOU: An Enneagram Journey to Discovering Personality Type, Self-Awareness, and Personal Growth."***

We are all searching for resolutions to the challenges we face. Even if we don't always communicate it directly, we all want to help ourselves and others and enjoy fuller, more satisfying lives. The Enneagram may not be able to solve every problem. Still, it can shine a light on why and how so many individuals inflict misery upon themselves and, by extension, others around them. The Enneagram personality types reveal the most prominent aspects of our inner geography, including the locations of our soul's perilous cliffs, deserts, and deadly quicksand, as well as its nourishing oases, tranquil forests, and revitalizing springs. We may choose whether or not to explore such depths, risk the pitfalls of emotional quicksand, or travel into uncharted territories. When the Enneagram is correctly understood and used, it becomes a map that shows us where we are in terms of our personalities and where we may go after we've gotten over ourselves.

Humans are incredibly complex, wonderful, infuriating, adaptable, and puzzling. It's as true about yourself as it is about the dozens of people you bump into daily. Every time you interact with others, you must operate on the often very limited knowledge you have about them.

And so much of it comes back to two fundamental problems:

We don't truly understand others.
We don't even truly understand ourselves.

This is why understanding personality can be so incredibly helpful. Personality typology is one of the personal and social constructs we've discovered to significantly influence our lives. No theory or framework can adequately describe or wholly account for who you are.

There are reasons why people behave the way they do.

Having a method to put those reasons into a more transparent system will allow you to grow your empathy and compassion for others. But much more importantly, understanding your reasons for doing what you do will grow compassion for yourself! And not just that, it will also give you the chance to do something about it.

Because you cannot change what you're not aware of.

This has made the Enneagram such a helpful tool for self-transformation for millions of people. The Enneagram is a personality typing system comprising nine unique personality types. It can be a valuable and profound tool for personal growth that helps build empathy and understanding for ourselves and others. The Enneagram invites us to look deeply into the mystery of our true identity. It is meant to initiate a process of inquiry that can lead us to a more profound truth about ourselves and our place in the world.

The Enneagram is best used as a guide to self-observation and self-inquiry. The Enneagram allows you to see some of the most difficult parts of yourself that you can't see without intentional reflection. It gives you a blueprint for understanding why you act the way you do. And if you can do the hard work and look at those blueprints, you will finally have what you need to begin growing in a long-lasting, transformative way.

This book will teach you:

- How to "observe and let go" of troublesome habits and reactions
- How to work with the motivations of each type
- Unconscious childhood messages
- Therapeutic strategies for each type
- How to cultivate awareness in your daily life
- How to use the system for continuing spiritual growth

This book will help you understand how you react to other people and experiences in your life and what those reactions tell you about your stress level and overall emotional health. When you understand yourself better, you can stop being controlled by fear and start living the life you desire.

It is time for us all to stop living in the past and realize our full potential. If you want to live an authentic life full of meaning and fulfillment, this book is for you! It will help you understand how your reactions to different situations can tell you about your overall emotional health and challenges. Utilize the information in this book to become the most improved version of yourself you can be. The world is counting on each of us to show up, to be less preoccupied with our egos, and to infect the social ecosystem with the most brilliant ideas we can muster.

Enjoy this free chapter!

I would like to ask a question—how would you characterize yourself? Who are you?

Since the beginning of human history, people have been hard at work developing personal and social constructs to define our personalities. These constructs consist of our many faiths, beliefs, meditative practices, and political structures. As a result, we arrange ourselves and our knowledge into what Timothy Leary would term "reality tunnels." These tunnels are our preferred ways of seeing the world, and we attempt to remain in harmony with these tunnels as much as possible.

We are all driven by a profound inner yearning. We may feel this yearning as a sense that something is missing in us, although it is usually difficult to define exactly what it is. We all have different ideas about what we think we need or want—a better relationship, a better job, a better body, a better home, and so on. We believe that if we get that perfect relationship or job or new "toy," the yearning will go away, and we will feel satisfied and complete. But experience teaches us that the new car makes us feel better for only a short time. The new relationship may be amazing, but it never quite fulfills us as we thought it would. So what are we really looking for? If we reflect for a moment, we may realize that what our hearts yearn for is to know who we are and why we are here. But little in our culture encourages us to hunt for answers to these essential questions. We've been brought up to believe that our exterior conditions will have the most impact on how happy we are. Sooner or later, however, we realize that superficial pleasures, while valuable in themselves, cannot address the deep restlessness of our soul. So, where can we look for answers?

Most personal development books on the market today focus primarily on the type of individuals we aspire to be. They recognize the vital importance of empathy, leadership, communication, and creativity. But as important and attractive as these (and other) qualities are, we find it extremely difficult to maintain them or to put them into practice in our daily lives. Our hearts yearn to soar, yet we almost always come crashing down painfully on the rocks of fear, self-defeating habits, and misinformation.

An effective approach to personal development must consider the fact that there are different kinds of people—different personality types. Personality typology is one of the personal and social constructs we've discovered to significantly influence our lives. No theory or framework can adequately describe or wholly account for who you are—the human species is too complicated to fit into one single framework, as there are so many things to be considered.

Learning about one facet of your personality doesn't magically reduce you to being only that aspect of yourself, any more than standing on a map would magically move you to a certain area. However, personality typology has proven to be one of the most valuable guides we've encountered in our search for self. Your personality might not be a direct indication of who you are, but it can serve as a map or guide to help you figure that out. And it is my conviction that our personalities may serve not only as a map to help us discover who we already are, but also as a manual to assist us in developing into the people we want to be.

No matter how well you're doing in life, the truth is that every person begins life affected in some way by the people around us and our experiences. And each one of us, consciously or unconsciously, covered over or clouded our true self, that fragrant essence of who we really are, devoid of all the clutter we picked up along the way.

This book will help you understand how you react to other people and experiences in your life and what those reactions tell you about your stress level and overall emotional health. When you understand yourself better, you can stop being controlled by fear and start living the life you desire.

Let's be honest—we're all a little lost sometimes. We go through life thinking that if we just had more money, more friends, or more time, everything would be okay. But the truth is that money, friends, and time are not what we need most. What we really need is to understand ourselves better.

Have you ever wondered why you sometimes feel stuck in the same patterns, repeating the same mistakes over and over? Or why sometimes you feel like you're constantly struggling to keep up with everyone else? It's because we've been indoctrinated with false beliefs about ourselves and our reality.

No matter where we come from, our false beliefs about ourselves and our reality greatly limit our growth and evolution. We become empowered by embracing our fears, uncovering false beliefs, and seeing others like us who have broken these patterns. We spend so much time trying to determine our personality type and how it affects us. We ask ourselves if we're extroverted or introverted, or if we're a thinker or a feeler. We ask ourselves where we fall on the spectrum of introversion/extroversion and whether we're more of a judger or a perceiver.

Because when you get down to it, all these labels—introvert/extrovert, thinker/feeler, judger/perceiver—are just constructs that we as humans have made up over time to try to understand ourselves and each other better. And while they might seem like helpful tools for understanding yourself, they can also blind you from seeing your full potential as a human being.

Coaching all over the world has taught me that we are all indoctrinated with false pretenses that do not serve us. We must break the old patterns and awaken to our true potential.

We are not our beliefs! When we believe this, we limit ourselves and others from experiencing the fullness of life. Our beliefs blind and limit us, holding us to a limited perspective. Our thoughts hold us back from experiencing life without limitations, without fear of judgment or failure, and without the need for approval. Our past and future thoughts keep us from enjoying the present moment.

We have the clarity to see through these false pretenses and what others are trying to teach us and mirror for us. We can step outside of this limited perspective with an awareness that allows us to grow into our fullest potential as human beings.

What if there were a system that could enable us to have more insight into ourselves and others? What if this system could show us our core psychological issues as well as our

strengths and weaknesses? What if this system did not depend on the assertions of experts or gurus, but on our personality patterns and willingness to explore ourselves honestly? What if this system showed us not only our core issues but also pointed out effective ways of dealing with them? Such a system exists, and it is called the Enneagram.

The Enneagram is a clear map of our souls for personal empowerment. It shows us exactly where we've been and where we're going in life—and helps us get there faster and with less struggle than ever before. In other words, it is a personality typology that maps the nine different types of personalities. Each type has its strengths and weaknesses, and each has its unique way of being in the world.

Knowing our type can help us discover how we operate in the world, why we do what we do, and what motivates us. The Enneagram is here to help you better understand yourself and live your best life! It can help us to understand ourselves, our relationships, and the world around us in a new way.

It's also an excellent tool for personal empowerment.

This tool helps us better understand the motives behind our behaviors by identifying nine different personality types. Each type has a unique way of approaching life and interacting with others. It is a tool to discover, understand, and live with our true selves. It's a modern tool that uses ancient ideas to help you take charge of your life.

The Enneagram shows us how to be better versions of ourselves by understanding what drives us, what holds us back, and how we can best use our strengths to help us achieve our goals. If you're a little confused right now, don't worry—that's all part of the process! The purpose of determining your Enneagram personality type is not to put yourself in a box but to identify the box you habitually put yourself in and step outside of it with awareness so that you can grow into your fullest potential as a human being.

Here's the gist—even with the most healthy, supportive parents on the planet, you will end up masking, suppressing, denying, or clouding parts of your true self or essence. Then you'll spend the rest of your life feeling like you're missing some important pieces of the puzzle you have become. Thus it becomes your lifelong quest to unveil your essence and become who you were meant to be. The Enneagram is a great road map to the treasures that lie inside you—unexpressed or expressed, conscious or unconscious, underutilized or unclaimed, and ripe with essence.

The veil becomes your personality and consists of what you think and feel and how you act or react to various life situations. The way you process information, as well as the way you characteristically behave, creates an amalgam of personality traits that define who you are. The Enneagram delineates nine core personality types and elucidates each type's primary fixations, motivations, and behavior patterns. Because everyone is born with certain affinities and is greatly affected by their formative years, variations within each type can be wide-ranging. Adult life experiences also affect personality alteration, accounting for swings in one direction or another. The Enneagram identifies nine core personalities based on the primary or predominant way people of each type emotionally experience, look at, and interact with the world around them. The Enneagram differs from other personality typing systems in that it doesn't describe our behaviors. There are stereotypical behaviors that align with each of the nine types, but the Enneagram is about our motivations—the *why* and *how* behind what we do. We all may exhibit the same behaviors, but the motivations behind those behaviors are often very different. Those motivations are what delineate the nine different types.

It's a natural human instinct to want to know more about ourselves. We want to understand who we are, why we are like this, how we got here, and how we can move forward. We strive to know ourselves a little bit more today than we did yesterday. You're not alone, and you no longer have to live with stress, anxiety, and fear. In this book, you'll learn how to understand your reactions to life events so that you can stop being controlled by fear and start living the life of your dreams.

One important idea in our understanding of the

Enneagram is the importance of self-awareness and introspection to progress toward personal growth and development. Acquiring in-depth knowledge of ourselves is the first step in altering our behavior and transcending our "false personality." Every spiritual journey begins with an individual's ability to transcend their ego, and the Enneagram reveals this process for each personality type. The Enneagram inspires us to explore ego transcendence and the integration of higher levels of consciousness by revealing the freer, broader dimensions of our own being and reassuring us that they are within our reach.

We are all searching for resolutions to the challenges we face. Even if we don't always communicate it directly, we all want to help ourselves and others and enjoy fuller, more satisfying lives. The Enneagram may not be able to solve every problem. Still, it can shine a light on why and how so many individuals inflict misery upon themselves and, by extension, others around them. The Enneagram personality types reveal the most prominent aspects of our inner geography, including the locations of our soul's perilous cliffs, deserts, and deadly quicksands, as well as its nourishing oases, tranquil forests, and revitalizing springs. We may choose whether or not to explore such depths, risk the pitfalls of emotional quicksand, or travel into uncharted territories. When the Enneagram is correctly understood and used, it becomes a map that shows us where we are in terms of our personalities and where we may go after we've gotten over ourselves.

If you want to live an authentic life full of meaning and fulfillment, this book is for you! It will help you understand how your reactions to different situations can tell you about your overall emotional health and challenges. Once you have that information, you can learn how to stop being controlled by fear and start living the life you desire.

The Enneagram helps us understand and express our innate individuality. We believe every person has a unique combination of characteristics, and we have created this book to help you find your unique mix. Determining our Enneagram personality type isn't meant to label us but rather to help us see the limitations of our worldview and break free of them so that we may develop to our maximum potential. In *The Art of Being You*, we'll help you discover what makes you YOU—and how to use those strengths to create the life YOU want!

It is time for us all to stop living in the past and realize our full potential. The Enneagram provides a transparent road map to our inner strengths and potential. Utilize the information in this book to become the most improved version of yourself you can be. The world is counting on each of us to show up, to be less preoccupied with our egos, and to infect the social ecosystem with the most brilliant ideas we can muster.

Get your full copy today! ***"THE ART OF BEING YOU: An Enneagram Journey to Discovering Personality Type, Self-Awareness, and Personal Growth."***

BOOKS BY RICHARD BANKS

Assertiveness Training: Learn How to Say No and Stop People-Pleasing by Establishing Healthy Boundaries

The Keys to Being Brilliantly Confident and More Assertive: A Vital Guide to Enhancing Your Communication Skills, Getting Rid of Anxiety, and Building Assertiveness

The Art of Active Listening: How to Listen Effectively in 10 Simple Steps to Improve Relationships and Increase Productivity

How to Deal With Stress, Depression, and Anxiety: A Vital Guide on How to Deal with Nerves and Coping with Stress, Pain, OCD and Trauma

How to Deal with Grief, Loss, and Death: A Survivor's Guide to Coping with Pain and Trauma, and Learning to Live Again

Develop a Positive Mindset and Attract the Life of Your Dreams: Unleash Positive Thinking to Achieve Unbound Happiness, Health, and Success

How to Stop Being Negative, Angry, and Mean: Master Your Mind and Take Control of Your Life

For the Full Book Listing go to https://author.to/RichardBanksBooks

REFERENCES

Brain Basics: Genes At Work In The Brain. (n.d.). National Institute of Neurological Disorders and Stroke. https://www.ninds.nih.gov/health-information/patient-caregiver-education/brain-basics-genes-work-brain

D. (2019, January 10). *Are you genetically predisposed to stress and anxiety?* https://www.dnafit.com/advice/stress-management/are-you-genetically-prone-to-stress-and-anxiety.asp

Davenport, C. (2022, February 22). *6 Superpowers Every Empath Possesses (and the 3 Things That Hold Us Back).* Medium. https://colettedavenport.medium.com/6-superpowers-every-empath-possesses-and-the-3-things-that-hold-us-back-87e4fdf26d68

Deschene, L. (2020, December 23). *10 Ways to Deal with Negative or Difficult People.* Tiny Buddha. https://tinybuddha.com/blog/how-to-deal-with-negative-people-or-difficult-people/

F. (2020, March 5). *The Difference Between Highly Sensitive People and Empaths*. Psychological and Educational Consulting. https://www.psychedconsult.com/the-difference-between-highly-sensitive-people-and-empaths/

Harris, D. W. (2021, December 17). *5 strategies for managing your emotions using emotional regulation.* CMHA National. https://cmha.ca/news/5-strategies-for-managing-your-emotions/

If You're a Highly Sensitive Person, You Experience the World Differently—Here's What It Means. (2022, December 6). Health. https://www.health.com/condition/mental-health-conditions/highly-sensitive-person-empath

Just a moment. . . (n.d.). https://www.choosingtherapy.com/highly-sensitive-person/

mindbodygreen. (2021, June 25). *The 5 Biggest Challenges Empaths Face In Romantic Relationships + How To Overcome Them.* Mindbodygreen. https://www.mindbodygreen.com/articles/problems-empaths-have-in-relationships

mindbodygreen. (2023, February 6). *Empaths In Love: How To Take Care Of Your Highly Sensitive Soul In Relationships*. Mindbodygreen. https://www.mindbodygreen.com/articles/dating-rules-for-empaths

Orloff, J. (2021, May 21). *Relationship Tips for Highly Sensitive People*. Judith Orloff MD. https://drjudithorloff.com/relationship-tips-for-highly-sensitive-people/

Parpworth-Reynolds, C. (2022, November 23). *10 Famous Empaths - Some Of These May Surprise You*. Subconscious Servant. https://subconsciousservant.com/famous-empaths/

Raypole, C. (2022, September 9). *15 Signs You Might Be an Empath*. Healthline. https://www.healthline.com/health/what-is-an-empath

Ryan, R. A. (2021, September 5). *What To Expect When Two Empaths Meet And Fall In Love*. YourTango. https://www.yourtango.com/experts/ronnieannryan/what-to-expect-when-two-empaths-fall-in-love

Staff, L. E. (2023, February 20). *The Importance of*

Empathy in the Workplace. CCL.
https://www.ccl.org/articles/leading-effectively-articles/empathy-in-the-workplace-a-tool-for-effective-leadership/

Stokes, V. (2021, April 6). *Intuitive Empaths: Signs, Types, Downsides, and Self-Care.* Healthline.
https://www.healthline.com/health/intuitive-empaths

Sutton, J., PhD. (2022, October 4). *How to Develop Empathy: 10 Exercises & Worksheets (+ PDF).* PositivePsychology.com.
https://positivepsychology.com/empathy-worksheets/

Timm, H. L., MA. (2021, October 26). *12 Self-Care Coping Skills for Empaths or HSP to Prevent Burn Out -.*
https://courageousandmindful.com/12-self-care-coping-skills-for-empaths-or-hsp-to-prevent-burn-out/

Why the World Needs an Empathy Revolution. (n.d.). Greater Good.
https://greatergood.berkeley.edu/article/item/why_the_world_needs_an_empathy_revolution

Wright, S. (2023, January 9). *Am I Highly Sensitive, and Empath, or Just Shy?* Perspectives Holistic Therapy.

https://www.perspectivesholistictherapy.com/blog-posts/2020/11/20/am-i-a-highly-sensitive-person-empath

Printed in Great Britain
by Amazon